NGÖNDRO

Ngöndro

THE FOUR FOUNDATIONAL PRACTICES
OF TIBETAN BUDDHISM

BUDDHIST MASTER
OLE NYDAHL

Preface by His Eminence Gyaltsab Rinpoche
Edited by Carol Aronoff

BLUE DOLPHIN PUBLISHING
1990

Other Books by Ole Nydahl

Entering the Diamond Way: My Path Among the Lamas
Basic Dharma
Practical Buddhism
Riding the Tiger (forthcoming)

For information, address
Blue Dolphin Publishing, Inc.
P.O. Box 1908
Nevada City, CA 95959

First printing: February, 1990

ISBN: 0-931892-23-6

Printed in the United States of America by
Blue Dolphin Press, Inc., Grass Valley, California

9 8 7 6 5 4 3 2 1

Table of Contents

Nov. 22, 1989

In order to develop the highest wisdom in our minds on the path, it is necessary to purify negative actions and obscurations and to accumulate merit, just as flowers cannot grow unless the ground is fertile and there is enough heat, humidity, sun etc.

The preliminary practices are methods which allow us, in the most efficient way, to purify negativity and accumulate merit.

This short and easily understandable text on the four preliminaries of Mahamudra has been composed by Ole Nydahl in order to benefit the dharma students by making this practice and its meaning accessible to them.

I am recommending followers of the Karma Kagyu School to read and use this book, and I am praying that it will be of great benefit for many beings.

Sincerely,

H.E. the 12th Goshir
Gyaltsab Drakpa Mingyur
Gocha.

Foreword

HERE, AT LAST, are the teachings on the foundational practices of Tibetan Buddhism in English. There is no substitute for these preliminaries; no other methods give a similar basis for continual and lasting growth. Teachers wanting to truly foster the development of their students will give these practices early before stiffness is produced by too much sitting meditation in one's untransformed state, or disillusionment occurs from doing advanced meditations one is not prepared for. Without the deep purification of these foundational practices and the resulting accumulation of confidence and psychological richness, neither sitting meditation nor the highest Yidam practices can ever be really effective.

The cultural jump from Tibet to the West of today is considerable, and is often rendered even more prohibitive by translations using fundamentalist Christian terminology which in no way reflects the Buddhist experience of spontaneous purity and freedom. For that reason I have written this commentary to the Root Text which will hopefully bring the precious tool of the Ngondro closer to you as the means to a better life, death, and rebirth.

Before beginning, you should obtain Refuge and the traditional transmission through hearing, or "lhung," from me or one of my colleagues in the Karma Kagyu lineage.

Also, make contact with one of our groups in order to obtain a copy of the Root-Text, and practice together where possible.

The Root-Text of the Ngondro which we have used is from: Kagyu Samye Ling, Tibetan Center, Eskdalemuir, Dumfriesshire, Scotland, U.K. You may obtain a copy by writng them directly, or from one of our groups.

As usual with my books, many share the merit. Edita Berger of our Hamburg Karma Kagyu Center collected lectures of mine for the German edition of this book. My secretary Maia Christensen compiled the Danish one and helped arrange many of the details for this edition. I spoke the translation onto a tape and Jaye Ito, Margaret Allsebrook, and Kathy Sullivan of the Marin Center in California, painstakingly typed and transcribed it all. As with all my work in English, Carol Aronoff gave invaluable help by editing the book. I would also like to thank Venora of Del Mar for her suggestions and Pam Steinmann of Fairfax, California for the final typing. And, of course, I must mention my friend Tomek Lehnert, who disturbed me all the time!!! I am very pleased that once again our publisher is Paul Clemens with Blue Dolphin.

OLE NYDAHL
Buddhist Master
Bodh Gaya, India,
Day of Mahakala, February 1989

Introduction to Ngondro

IT IS IMPOSSIBLE TO OVERESTIMATE the value of the Ngondro, the four foundational practices of Tibetan Buddhism. In a direct and very practical way, these preliminary practices bring forth our potential while removing the veils which keep us from experiencing and expressing our Enlightened nature. What especially hinders us is the mind's tendency to cling to its constantly changing impressions. For example, though we may not have experienced any anger five minutes earlier, and it will most likely be gone five minutes later, our mind still treats the feeling as if it were substantial and real. It then acts from that basis, setting things in motion in the outer world as well as planting seeds in its store-consciousness which will bring about suffering in the future. This cycle, which is largely out of one's control, is the normal state of most beings; people are not free to choose what they wish to experience.

The Buddha's goal, then, is to enable us to know that freedom which we've actually *always* had, to help beings experience the open, clear, unobstructed nature of mind. He shows us that its timeless essence is perfect: open like space, radiantly intelligent and alive, and without any limits; that although intangible and not a thing in itself, still it is capable of experiencing and knowing all things. Resting in this primordial awareness brings fearlessness, spontaneous joy and active compassion; it is perfection itself.

The Buddha advised three steps for realizing this state. On the outer level, he stressed intelligent use of the law of cause and effect. For people of greater maturity, he gave the inner teachings of compassion and wisdom. And to those with spontaneous confidence in their own Buddha-nature, he taught the special methods which work from the absolute level, enabling one to identify with Enlightenment, to experience timeless truth directly.

Important on all levels is the understanding that things and our conditioned states of mind have no enduring independent nature, but instead consist of conditions which come together temporarily, change and dissolve. Our subjective experience of what happens and our judgments and reactions are thus not based on something truly existing out there, but are colored by our varying states of mind. A frequent quote in Buddhist texts is: "Everything looks yellow to the jaundiced eye."

There are two ways to view this. The wrong way is to see emptiness as nothingness or a black hole, while the right understanding, seeing space as alive, and intelligent and rich, removes all suffering and brings forth our full freedom and joy.

The way there requires "Two Accumulations." The first, Sonam Kyi Tsog, is the accumulation of positive impressions/merit in our store consciousness, providing a foundation of powerful, good impressions manifesting both internally and externally. As long as we are still attached to changing and impermanent experiences, it is better that these be at least pleasant, while for Enlightenment, positive impressions are a must. Without them the mind will not develop the joyful confidence to start discovering itself.

The second accumulation, known as Yeshe Kri Tsog in Tibetan, is the development of wisdom. This is not the knowledge acquired in school. It doesn't consist of putting more information into the mind, but, rather, on relaxing and intuitively experiencing things the way they *really* are, beyond concepts, without expectations or fear.

Mind in its true essence is uncontrived and timeless. It would be experienced that way if its impressions weren't forced into systems of judgment and evaluation. What makes our actions pure is our contact with this underlying essence. The accumulation of good impressions produces spontaneous insight, which then motivates more positive actions and, the resulting growth allows us to see things ever more as they are. Without filters, we can work directly with what's there.

In order to enhance and secure our development, the ninth Karmapa, Wangchug Dorje, gave the *Chag Chen Ngondro*. The goal of its four practices is the realization of Mahamudra, the highest insight, and the name "Chag Chen Ngondro" means "the preparatory way to Mahamudra." In each of the four practices, this highest realization serves as the basis, the way and the goal. The process is the same: first we open our body, speech and mind to aspects of Enlightenment, knowing that they are no different from our own true nature. Then we practice the repetitions, the physical exercises, visualizations and mantras which make them come alive. Finally, we merge with them, manifesting fully their Enlightened energy. The power of our mind to do this lifts all experience to the level of a Pure Land, a state of mind where all things are seen in a jovial light and further our growth. Building increasing levels of good Karma and insight, the Ngondro thus leads us to the ultimate wisdom of Mahamudra.

The first preliminary, Refuge with prostrations, aims at clearing away obscurations and accumulating good impressions. It is a very physical and powerful practice, focusing mainly on activities of the body.

The second foundation, Dorje Sempa, purifies our speech and mind and develops both merit and insight, though mostly the former. Dreams and daily experiences will already begin to reflect greater wisdom. Life will still be taken quite personally, but moments of space and clarity will grow more frequent.

In the third practice, Mandala offerings, wisdom and merit are equally emphasized. We understand that the Refuge to which we make offerings and our own essence are really one. Here, the unity of subject, object and action becomes much clearer.

The last foundation, Guru Yoga, is basically the Three Lights meditation preceded by a number of prayers. It primarily develops our wisdom. The purification from the first two practices along with the inner richness produced by the Mandala offerings make possible the timeless merging of the Buddha's body, speech and mind with our own. Through this, glimpses of intuitive wisdom begin to really affect our lives, becoming more constant as we progress along the path.

If we have confidence in our inherent truth nature, and in the 2,500 years of unbroken Buddhist experience, we'll find that the use of these repetitions, digging out the roots of ignorance again and again, is the best way to bring forth our Enlightened essence. Even the wisest and most convincing thoughts are like bubbles in the air when we die; they cannot help us. On the other hand, strong dharmic habits influencing our totality will not only help us in this life, but also at and after death.

At that time, when sense impressions stop and both habitual tendencies and the timeless Buddha energies of our mind awaken, we can then recognize those aspects we have meditated on and merge with them at a level beyond time and place. Just as mental disturbances consist of repetitive patterns, so repetition is also the antidote which removes them. Through constantly hitting in the same place until the veils of ignorance have been pierced, the mind's steady power begins to manifest naturally.

Four times 111,111 repetitions (of Refuge and prostrations, Dorje Sempa, Mandala offerings and Guru Yoga) thus cut away countless hindrances and prepare us for the direct experience of our primordial nature. Ordinarily, when we try to meditate, our mind wanders or gets dull. Even if we sit for long periods in the same place, this lack of clarity and concentration remains. We will see that there isn't much value in just sitting in one's unreformed state, that it makes people robot-like or dependent. That is why Shamata (or Shinay, in Tibetan) was not given in authentic Tibetan Buddhism until after the Ngondro was completed or, in rare cases, alongside it. We have here an important reason why maturity, freshness and flexibility characterize those who follow the traditional way.

How then do we practice? We work in an integrated way with body, speech and mind, using these very effective tools. If our mind strays from the Buddha aspect, we hold it with the energy of the mantras. If this is also difficult, we shift our emphasis to the senses of the body, focusing on the prostrations, on the mala in our hand or, eventually, on the experience of our Buddha body and its energy-channels. This prevents stiffness and discouragement, and makes the best possible use of our time.

CHAPTER ONE

Prostrations, with Refuge and Bodhisattva Prayers

PROSTRATIONS ARE THE FIRST of these preliminary meth-ods. We begin by taking Refuge, and what is most important here is *where* we look for that refuge. If we seek security in impermanent things like money, status, youth or beauty, we will have empty hands one day, with no dividends coming in. If, however, we take Refuge in the timeless nature of mind, we'll find something which is endlessly rich and can never disappear. This is the reason we practice.

The steps of the Ngondro were given by the Buddha 2,500 years ago, and we find them practiced as a total system about 500 years later at Nalanda University in India. Between 700 and 1,000 A.D., when the Buddhist culture was destroyed in India as a result of several Muslim invasions, those people who held methods of the Diamond Way managed to take them over the Himalayas into Tibet. The first to do this was the famous Guru Rinpoche, Padma-sambhava, who arrived around 740 A.D. After him, Yeshe Tsogyal, his main consort, carried the teachings on until King Langdarma destroyed the transmission. He reinstated

the old shamanistic religion of Bon, which was native to
Tibet, and little but the Termas, the purposefully "Hidden
Teachings," were left.

The renewal of Buddhism came through Marpa, "the
translator." During the period 950-1,000 A.D., he went to
India three times. He spent a total of sixteen years there,
and brought back to Tibet the most powerful Tantric
teachings. Since then, the Ngondro has been an inseparable
part of the practice lineages in Tibet. There are some
Tibetans who have done the complete practices up to
twenty-five times, and one can really feel that. Others may
be more articulate, but these people don't need to prove
anything. They are unshakeable, like rocks. Kalu Rinpoche
says it this way: "A sock will not become clean by dipping it
into water once, but if you do it often, there will be results."

In the West, we have better powers of concentration
than people who have not gone to school. Also, collective
experience and good communication has inoculated us
against many of the confusions people in other cultures are
now falling prey to en masse. As a result, we may not need
twenty-five Ngondros, but one is necessary; there is no help
to be found in clever ideas when sickness, old age and death
come near. Our only refuge then is the work we have done
with our mind. The Buddhist Ngondro in particular gives
us a strong personal refuge in our beingness and mind.

This work is strengthened through the blessings of the
Lama and, especially inside our Karma Kagyu lineage, one
can hitchhike a good part of the way to enlightenment. If
we open up to the power of the Karmapas, it is possible to
remove the disturbing habits and imprints from countless
lives in just a few years. Without practice, however, it is

difficult to hold this power. Only through hard work can we transform ourselves in a lasting way.

Many people think they can meditate directly on the mind, but for a long while until the mind is very finely tuned, that isn't true. Whoever analyzes, during a period of meditation, how much of that time the mind actually experiences inspiration, joy and peace will find, to their amazement, that it is, at the most, only a few minutes. The rest of the time one is pulled here and there by feelings and thoughts, or wanders in the future or the past. In the beginning it is not enough to just sit. What our practice should bring about is not a "white wall" samadhi where one is outwardly meditating but inwardly asleep. The goal here is not to kill thoughts or freeze the mind. According to Kalu Rinpoche, this kind of "calming" actually lowers our intelligence and may even bring about rebirth as a big fish, while our wish instead is to unfold the mind's spontaneous compassion, fearlessness, and joy.

Ngondro, on the other hand, which employs specific methods to accumulate positive impressions and wisdom, makes our mind like a diamond: radiant and clear. The way of Vajrayana includes skillful means and the full development of our potential, the purification of body, speech and mind.

We start our practice with the prostrations, primarily activating the body and its inner channels. Here, in brief, is what we actually do:

We feel the formless stream of air, coming and going at the tips of our noses. We just let all thoughts and ideas go by, without holding onto them.

Then we think of the four basic thoughts which
motivate us to become enlightened: 1) We think about the
precious opportunity in this life, here and now, to
consciously work with our mind for the benefit of others
and ourselves. 2) We remember the impermanence of
everything conditioned, understanding that the only thing
which can never disappear is the open, clear limitless mind
which is aware now. 3) We realize that we create our reality
and think about cause and effect, knowing that our former
actions, words and thoughts have become our world of
today and at this very moment we sow the seeds for our
future. 4) Finally we work with the mind because we are of
little use to others while still confused and suffering
ourselves. Because we are unable to hold our mind the way
we wish, we want to learn from those who can teach us how.

After contemplating the four thoughts to turn the
mind, we focus on the Refuge. While reading through the
text, we open ourselves to the Lama (Karmapa), surrounded by the Lineage, to the Yidams, the Buddhas, the
teachings, the practicing ones and the powerful Protectors.
We think of all beings around us, known as well as
unknown, and while holding the image of the Refuge tree
in our mind as well as we can (or looking at a representation
of it in front), we repeat the six lines of the Refuge prayer,
taking care not to disturb others. In time, our visualization
will become stronger, and it will be like prostrating in front
of your lama with the whole lineage tree vibrantly present
smiling upon you.

With the palms of our hands pressed together, we first
touch the crown of our head where nerves, senses and the
brain are located (symbolizing the body); then our throat
(center of speech and communication), and finally the heart

SIX-LINE REFUGE PRAYER
(Said while doing prostrations)

Palden lama dam pa nam la kyab su chio
Yidam kyil khor gyi lha tsog nam la kyab su chio
Sang gye chom den de nam la kyab su chio
Dam pai chö nam la kyab su chio
Pag pai gen dun nam la kyab su chio
Pa wo kha dro chö kyong sung mai tsog yeshe kyi
   chen dang den pa nam la kyab su chio

We go for refuge to all the splendid accomplished
   supreme gurus.
We go for refuge to all the yidams, the deities gathered
   in the mandala.
We go for refuge to all Buddhas, the transcendent
   accomplished conquerors.
We go for refuge to all the supreme Dharma.
We go for refuge to all the noble Sangha.
We go for refuge to all the dakas, dakinis, protectors
   and defenders of the Dharma who each have the eye
   of transcending awareness.

center in the middle of the chest where strong feelings and
states of inspiration are experienced (it is for this reason
that we think of the mind as being there).

In this way, we and all beings open our three upper
centers while repeating the six lines and sliding out to our
full length. It's good to let our hands touch thumb against
thumb when we're fully stretched out, and we count the
prostrations rather than the Refuge prayers. We repeat the

six line prayer in the way which feels best, either flowing continually, which gives us two to three prostrations for each recitation of the prayer, or, if it's difficult initially to remember the six lines while there is so much else to learn, we can use a technique which evolved in our Hamburg center. First, they do one prostration for each line and then gradually get into a more natural rhythm.

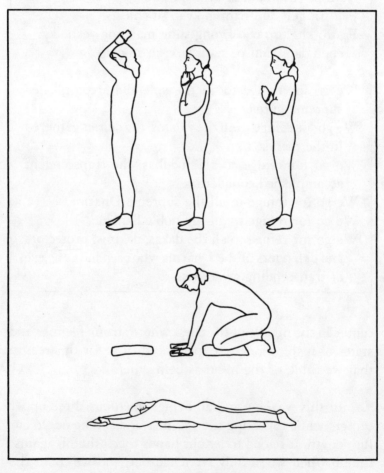

Full-length Prostrations

While we slide out to our full length again and again, some important processes may occur. In the mind, strong devotion may arise, a feeling of coming home. Our mind begins to understand that it's our own Enlightened nature we're prostrating to, while the energies of our body are straightened and blockages fall away. This is especially useful for those of us of the drug generation who often played more with inner energies than our untrained systems could always handle. The result was much too often spiritual pride, wrong views, inflexible minds or even madness, and nothing eliminates old damage or ticking time bombs better than this most physical of practices.

When one has finished the 111,111 prostrations, something has happened. The body is no longer a hindrance, a thing one has to drag around. Instead, it has become a pleasant tool and a useful servant to the mind. It functions with less drama and can contain more joy. One may now experience waves of blessing and states of psychological richness, and feel grateful for no reason at all.

There is one obstacle on our way, however, which some mistakenly think of as growth. It is that nauseating quality called false spirituality, where the ego turns everything to its own advantage. It takes two words from one religion, half an experience from somewhere else, and mixes everything in such a way as to inflate its own position. It will neither discriminate nor learn from experience. Though prostrations in sufficient quantities are an effective antidote, still, please beware. Nothing befits a yogi less than this sugary vibration, and expressions like: "it is all from God, and it is all the same," are the clearest sign of superficiality.

Also in Buddhist practice, the ego is first led to believe that its field is being enlarged, and one thinks things like, "Before I was a success and now I am also becoming spiritual"—otherwise we could never start—but the practice is actually designed to dig the soil away from the ego's roots, to make us spontaneous and effortless here and now. As we continue on our way, devotion and openness will inevitably appear, removing contrived states of mind; it can't be avoided. Also, the Refuge prayers produce effects on more than just the level of words and thoughts. They awaken unconditioned states of confidence, joy and love which gradually become our constant state. Again, due to the great number of repetitions, they make us transcend personal and cultural limitations.

We can only expect deep and lasting benefit when we hold the highest motivation, that of reaching Enlightenment for the good of all beings. That way, we cannot go wrong. It is best to follow the steps of the traditional text, and although some of its imagery may be foreign to us, it is part of a complete psychological laboratory which has been effective for the last 2,500 years in producing enlightenment.

To build up lasting power for our meditation, it is essential to first understand where we are right now, and here I want to backtrack to our motivation for any kind of Buddhist practice, the Four Thoughts which also precede the prostrations. The first thing we contemplate is our precious opportunity to become enlightened for the good of all. Very few have the good karma to meet with undiluted truth. It seems that the more superficial a teacher is, and the more he takes advantage of people's confusion by teaching the latest fads or telling them what they would like to hear, the more people go to him, at least till the bubble bursts. The higher and more vast the teachings, not just on the level of ideas, but concerning the direct experience of the timeless mind, the less people manage to make a connection. "There is much iron but little gold," the Tibetans say, and they traditionally explain it like this:

Eighteen conditions must come together for a precious human life to arise. Here first, the eight things which prevent the practice of Dharma:

Taking birth in
    the hell realms (states of extreme paranoia)
    the ghost realms (states of extreme greed and attachment)
    the animal realms (states of laziness and confusion)
    the gods' realms (where there is no spiritual motivation),
Being born as a barbarian in a land without Dharma,
Being born as a being who cannot appreciate the Dharma even when exposed to it,
Being born in dark times when no Buddhas appear,
Being born with such mental or bodily impairments that one cannot understand or practice the teachings.

Having attained a human birth free of the eight hindrances, we then need ten opportunities to be able to practice. Five conditions are brought about by others: (1) in spite of many difficulties, the Buddha Shakyamuni took birth in our historical time, and (2) gave the teachings; (3) the Dharma is still being taught, and (4) is given life today by the practitioners, and (5) generous people who support the Dharma.

The last five conditions we create through our own Karma: We need (1) a body free of the eight unfavorable conditions. We must (2) be born in or visit a place where the teachings can be obtained; (3) our sense organs must not be so damaged that we cannot understand the things taught. We must (4) not be influenced by people with wrong views concerning the Buddhist path, and (5) we must have a deep confidence in the Buddha, his teachings and the practicing ones.

Only when these eighteen conditions come together do we have the precious human body which is the basis for lasting development. It is said that it is difficult to become a millionaire, but that is nothing compared to what it takes to really grow through a liberating practice.

The next view to work into our system is the realization of the impermanence of all things. We see that the precious opportunity we have now won't always be there, and that being born, we shall inevitably die. The only uncertainty is when. Noticing how seconds become minutes, minutes hours, hours days, and so on, we become interested in the only thing which cannot die, change or disappear: the open, clear, limitless nature of the mind, which we want to realize as quickly as possible, before our opportunity is lost.

The third thing to understand is Karma, the chain of cause and effect in which we are now caught. Whatever we do, say, or think will become our future; even our current situation now is conditioned by our past. Until we attain liberation or Enlightenment, we have only limited freedom. Even though the impressions in our mind change constantly, we are still taken in and pulled along by them, creating confusion and suffering. The examples of the Buddha and, more recently, the Karmapas show that full Enlightenment exists, and that we can have complete confidence in the open space of mind; its essence is perfection. After some time of practice, our awareness increases of how cause and effect operate in the outer world, and we begin to see similar processes at work in our own lives, which is the first step towards gaining control. We develop an inner sensitivity on many levels; as long as we act from the general feeling of oneness with others, no inner alarms will go off, while any physical sign of mounting aggression will be relayed directly to our awareness, which then helps diminish our habit of repeating the same mistakes. In the free space obtained, we gradually learn to plant the seeds for what we wish to happen in the future.

The last point to turn our mind is why there is no alternative to a life of awareness—why should we do a difficult practice like the Ngondro? And here, a Westerner may find the text a little theatrical. It's written for another culture and contains references to executioners, places of execution and other exotic things. If, however, we look at the meaning rather than the images, it makes good, common sense.

The reasons for practicing Dharma should be woven as deeply into our lives as possible. If we want the stolid horse of our habitual mind to move, it is best to sometimes hold a carrot in front of its nose and a whip at its behind. Motivating ourselves *often* is important. I advise focusing on the carrot in front as much as possible, recognizing that Enlightenment is more intensely joyful and powerful than anything we know today, that it is completely uncondi-tioned and can never disappear. All who realize the essence of the mind say the same thing: there are no words to express the joy of Enlightenment. It's not the same as having the experience oneself, of course, but what we do know from our present lives points in the same direction. Those moments of deepest joy when everything is suddenly radiant and fresh and totally new appear when the mind experiences peace, not when we feed it impressions. This logically means that such states can be made constant and lasting. The essential thing is knowing that mind, in itself, is the highest joy, uncontrived, timeless and perfect, and that Buddhist practice will infallibly bring us there. Beyond dreams and artificiality, there is a truth more wonderful than anything we can imagine.

So use the carrot, stressing joy, but when it doesn't motivate enough, the whip becomes useful. This consists of understanding our situation. Unless we realize the timeless nature of our mind, we will continue to think that we are our body, and that feelings and possessions are ours. Believing this, like all beings who don't have lasting spiritual values, we'll suffer from inevitable loss, sickness, old age, and death, thinking that it happens to "us."

Three kinds of suffering exist until Enlightenment is attained. First, there is the rough type where everything breaks down or dies and we become totally neurotic. Second, there is the more subtle kind associated with change; neither our interest in external phenomena nor the things themselves will last. And third, there is the all-pervasive experience of being ignorant, of not knowing what is really happening. One or more of these sufferings will be with us until Enlightenment is reached. Carrot and whip together thus bring us the fourth basic understanding of why we seek Enlightenment.

If we examine our changing states of mind, we will see that they constantly color our experience. When we are doing well, the world seems beautiful, and everything has meaning, but when we are angry or feeling badly, people have fangs, and everything seems ugly and gray. It is not the world changing, however, but rather our own mind. People's particular veils, expectations, and ripening Karmas cause them to experience things so differently.

Only at the highest levels of realization do we fully transcend seeing the world through distortions of rosy or dark-colored glasses. Only there do we stop separating things according to what we like or don't like. At these levels, the projections disappear along with our attachment and ill will, and, for the first time, we see how things really are. We need only to remove ignorance in order to experience the Pure Land, to let self-evident truth, wisdom, power and joy appear as the true nature of things. We don't need to die in order to get there, or to go somewhere to meet Buddhas; all beings have the Buddha nature; they just haven't realized it yet.

While seeing blissful truth on the absolute level, we remember that things function on the relative plane as well. We are clear, confident and unsentimental, and we don't make mistakes. The highest, purest levels of experience which arise during meditation are not an exchange of bad pictures in the mirror for good ones, which are equally conditioned and impermanent. Instead, they are a growing taste of that timeless state where the clear, radiant, wise and compassionate space of the mirror recognizes itself.

In Vajrayana, the Diamond Way, this goal is obtained through identifying with the pure levels of consciousness expressed by the Karmapa's Black Crown, the Refuge Tree, Dorje Sempa, the Mandala we offer to, and so on. Merging with these Enlightened aspects, the mind stops distinguishing between truth inside and out. The mind, although "empty of" color, weight, form or smell, and unable to see itself from anywhere else—both the seer and the thing looked for are the mind—still it can experience its own perfection as the different Buddhas—forms of energy and light—and become aware of their richness, as when looking into a mirror and finally realizing its oneness with them. Resting in itself and identifying with the timeless power, compassion, joy and wisdom which the forms embody, nothing then is needed but to be natural. Seeing that all beings want to experience happiness and avoid suffering, we work intuitively and effortlessly, realizing that we can only manifest our own maturity and fearlessness.

This first outline was intended to "anchor down" the view which keeps us motivated to practice. Now we come to the awareness to be held during the prostrations.

First, we appear in a beautiful meadow with soft, springy grass, surrounded by all sentient beings. Traditionally, we imagine our father to our right and our mother to our left, whether they are alive or not, and around them are all the beings we know or can imagine, countless, and of every kind. They all look in the same direction as ourselves, and collectively we deeply wish to reach the state beyond all suffering and confusion.

In front of us is a radiant, beautiful lake. The water is cool, delicious, light, soft, clear, free of impurities, and harmful neither to the throat nor to the stomach.

In its middle stands a wish-fulfilling tree, a perfect shape of energy and light, and where the golden trunk separates into four silver branches, sits our direct contact with Enlightenment, the Lama. For us in the Karma Kagyu tradition, he is always His Holiness, the Karmapa, manifesting either in his physical form with the Black Crown, or as Dorje Chang, a seated Buddha of blue light holding dorje and bell, his arms crossed at his heart (see front cover).

If we are able to see the Karmapa as a form of energy and light, then the jump to the level where everything is pure will be short, and all enlightened qualities will appear in us naturally. If, on the other hand, we experience him as a man with a liver and kidneys, as somebody too thick or too thin, it is better to focus on Dorje Chang. The jump from there to the experience of purity here and now is in that case somewhat greater, but we have to do what we can. "Meditating on the Lama is like meditating on 100,000 Buddha forms," Naropa said, and in all successful Karma Kagyu centers, identification with the Karmapa is the central practice.

The important thing to know is that Dorje Chang is Karmapa's mind and that Karmapa is Dorje Chang's body. Being king of Tibetan yogis, the first incarnate Lama and leader of the most important Kagyu schools, the Karmapa holds every living transmission and carries the unbroken Enlightenment of all Buddhas right up to the present time.

Around him, as the living foliage of the tree, is the whole lineage: the former incarnations of the Karmapa and those incarnations of the Sharmapa, Situ, Gyaltsap and Jamgon Kongtrul Rinpoches who have held the transmission between the Karmapas until today. They are, respectively, the emanations of Opame (Amitabha), Maitreya,

Vajrapani and Manjushri, and these have alternated with
the Karmapa as holders of the lineage since 1193.

The uppermost Buddha on the tree is Dorje Chang,
timeless Enlightenment itself. This principle is expressed
in the old transmission lineage through the Buddha
Kuntuzangpo, the All Good. He and Kuntuzangmo, his
consort, are the truth of the truth state, while Dorje Chang
is its joy. His ornaments show the freshness and bliss of
Enlightenment. The bell he holds is the female aspect,
space, high intuitive wisdom and the Buddha's speech and
body, while the dorje represents the male aspect, bliss,
highest compassion, skillful means and the Buddha mind.

Underneath Dorje Chang, depending on whether the
tree shows the transmission of the Six Doctrines (the
realization of the mind through its clarity or energy) or that
of Mahamudra (the realization of the mind through its
space and awareness which this practice aims at), one sees
either the Indian yogis Tilopa and Naropa or, in the present
case, Lodro Rinchen, Saraha, Nagarjuna, Shavaripa and
Maitripa. Dorje Chang always comes first. Below the
Indians, sits Marpa, a mountain of power, who brought
both the Mahamudra and the Six Doctrines to Tibet, and
below him are Milarepa, Gampopa and the first Karmapa,
Dusum Khyenpa. All the other Karmapas are also present,
along with the high incarnate Lamas between them. Thus,
the foliage of the tree is the place from whence experience
and blessings derive, opening us, removing blocks and
doubts, and giving us the confidence necessary for growth.

The Refuge Tree, however, is more than just blessing.
It's also liberating inspiration and spiritual power, which
manifest through the Yidams on the branch stretching

towards us. "Yi" means "mind" and "dam" means "bond." Thus, the Yidam is a Buddha aspect which connects our mind with Enlightenment. Regardless of our inner tendencies, whether we are plagued by confusion, attachment,

anger or all together, these peaceful, wrathful or united forms of light and energy manifest the potential of our mind on the level of Enlightenment. Identifying with them over and over again effectively diminishes the limiting influences of our solid body and its sensory impressions, and as the free energy of our mind increases, and the refuse of disturbing feelings turns to compost, fantastic trees and flowers begin to grow where, earlier, we had to hold our noses.

Looking at the branch stretching towards us, we see, centrally, Demchok or Chakrasamvara (Sanskrit), the most important Yidam of our Karma Kagyu lineage. He is blue, has two, ten or sixteen arms, and denotes timeless highest bliss, a state reached only through the experience of non-ego and emptiness. For this, we meditate on Dorje Phagmo, his consort, a more or less wrathful figure, red, naked and in the dancing posture. She brings us the radiant awareness of the mind, its transparency and playful perfection.

There are other Yidams on the branch as well. Very important are Gyalwa Gyamtso, a red Chenrezig sitting in union, and also other united forms in different colors, like the wonderful Taras. The Yidams of the highest Anuttara-tantra class are always in union, because only there are compassion and wisdom, bliss and space fully integrated.

Aspects like Chenrezig, Tara and Manjushri may manifest as Yidams, Bodhisattvas or Buddhas, depending on our need. In our lineage, the Yidam is that aspect of the Karmapa one has the closest connection to, one side of the radiant jewel of his mind. You can also meditate on one of his incarnations, as he told Hannah and me to do.

To the left of the tree, seen from our perspective, is the branch with the Buddhas. Depending on the tradition and artist's preference, their number may vary. If there are ten, they symbolize the spacious nature of Enlightenment: the four cardinal points, the four intermediate points, zenith and nadir. If there are three, they are the Buddhas of past, present and future in protective, teaching and earth-touching postures. And if there's only one form, it is the Buddha-essence itself, the open, clear, unlimited nature of mind.

Behind the tree is a branch which is not visible to the eye, "but can be known by the mind," as Kalu Rinpoche says. To the left and right of the tree, we may see the corners of a great stack of books which sit on this branch and contain the Dharma. Here we should not think of an enormous amount of printed paper, but of a living transmission of enlightening experience. We can imagine the full Kangyur, the 108 volumes containing the 84,000 liberating teachings which the Buddha gave. We can also think of three books, one on top of the other, containing the teachings of the Hinayana, the Mahayana, and with the Vajrayana on top. Or, we may imagine only one book, the essence of it all. In order to make it less dry—and the tree is very male—we can also meditate on a yellow, immensely beautiful female Buddha form, the Prajnaparamita, the highest wisdom of the Buddhas, with her hands in the teaching mudra.

To the right, also from our perspective, is the branch with the Sangha, the practicing ones. There we find the Bodhisattvas, Enlightened energies who are active in this world and take rebirth as natural leaders for the benefit of all. They accompany beings on their way and help us, either through direct physical contact or as a positive and guiding influence.

There are many teachings about Buddhas and Bodhisattvas and their respective power and levels of attainment. To avoid confusion, however, it's easiest to see them as Buddhas when they show the goal, and as Bodhisattvas when they help us on the way, to differentiate them according to their function. The three main Bodhisattvas, mentioned below, are both Buddhas and Yidams, and their protective emanations are the two-, four- and six-armed Mahakalas.

The central Bodhisattva on the branch is Chenrezig or Avalokiteshvara (Skt.), the condensed love and compassion of all Buddhas. His name in Tibetan means "compassionate eyes," and he is most often shown in his white four-armed form with lotus, crystal mala and the jewel of the mind in his hands.

To one side is Jampeyang (or Manjushri), the highest wisdom of all Buddhas. He is orange and holds up a two-edged sword, cutting through all the veils of ignorance. His left hand holds a lotus flower which opens at his left ear, and carries the book containing all wisdom. To the other side is Chana Dorje (or Vajrapani), the power of all Buddhas and the "father" of two-armed Mahakala. In the Pho-Wa I teach, he emanates in his light blue peaceful aspect, holding bell and dorje, while usually he manifests in his dark blue, powerful form surrounded by flames. At first glance, he looks like the protectors, but his ornaments are jewels and not bones. He expresses the *energy* of Enlightenment. We may also find the other Mahabodhisattvas like Kshitigarbha, Sarvanivarna Vishkambhin, Akashagarbha, Maitreya, Vajrapani and Samantabhadra, but if only one is portrayed, it is always Chenrezig. Compassion is most important of all.

Between the four branches and the water of the lake underneath is the blue-black power-field of the Mahakalas and other protectors. From it, flames shoot out in all directions, fangs and weapons flash, and power-sounds like "Hung," "Rulu," "Jo" and "Pe" vibrate loudly. The protectors are the activities of Buddhas who roll up their sleeves in order to keep hindrances and suffering away. They all have the wisdom eye in their forehead which shows they are not demons or other negative energies, and the faster the pace of our development, the more we need them.

The main protector of our lineage is the two-armed Mahakala, Bernak Chen, the "bearer of the black coat." His energy is so powerful that it cannot be described directly, only through its various signs and attributes. His head is one-third of his total height and his fangs are bared. He has three bloodshot eyes and heavy-set, muscular arms and legs. Underneath the black coat, he wears the bone ornaments of great bliss, and his right hand holds a chopping knife which cuts away all hindrances, while the skull bowl in his left hand contains the lifeblood and heart of the ego. His powerful feet trample attachment and ill will. The sun disc underneath represents highest awakened wisdom, and the flames around him express the intensity of his compassion. He is shown in the center of the cloud of protectors, either alone or with his consort, Palden Lhamo, on a mule. For the sake of visual contrast, on some paintings you will see his coat painted green.

To the right and left are the other protectors, the four and six-armed Mahakalas, Dorje Legpa, Shing Kyong, Dorje Phurba, Namtose, Dzambala, Guru Dragpo, Dukar and others, the forces who make the Diamond Way possible. Each one has general protective power as well as a special field of activity, and there is no way we can overestimate their importance.

This whole field of Enlightenment is our Refuge, and we open body, speech and mind to its six aspects by prostrating and reciting the six-line invocation. In order to increase the effect on our mind, we can imagine ourselves in hundreds or thousands of forms and be aware of all the beings around us doing prostrations as well. Thus, our collective search for happiness gives power to our practice and, at the same time, removes all feelings of separation. We become like an ocean where the waves naturally and joyfully beat against the shore.

From the tree, lights of many colors stream into us. We hear beautiful music, or syllables of power, and smell lovely fragrances. The openness to Enlightenment we develop here provides a solid foundation for all future practice. It's not easy, however. When we do prostrations and the body hurts, the ego tries to protect itself through resistance, disease and doubt. Our parents and friends often don't like what we do, considering us exotic or guru-damaged. If we remember, however, that this practice has given beings the power to help others for 2,500 years, we'll persevere, and if nothing else works, one can always hint that it costs a lot of money to learn. Then everyone will have respect!

There is no better support for our practice than the power of habit and the understanding of how privileged we really are. It will keep our motivation from becoming abstract or lukewarm.

Sometimes, it's good to retreat for a weekend in order to do as many prostrations as we can. This renews and deepens our experience. Also, don't think too much about the number of repetitions or of finishing them. It will only make you feel you aren't getting anywhere. Don't think, "I'll be finished soon and then something fantastic will occur—a beautiful meditation, or whatever." Instead, just feel good about what happens in the moment and see the prostrations as the very important practice of body, speech and mind that they are. This view will bring the most benefit.

When we've done as many prostrations as we can, we then get into the position we know from the Refuge and Bodhisattva vows, kneeling with the right knee down and the left knee up, pressing our hands together at the heart. In front of the whole Refuge tree, we now take the Bodhisattva vow (p. 40), promising to reach Enlightenment quickly so we can benefit all beings.

After that, we sit normally and read through the rest of the text. We understand that now we've become the Buddha's son or daughter and that it's important to preserve the good style of this noble family. We again wish all beings happiness, that their wishes may be fulfilled.

Last is the prayer which evokes the four immeasurable qualities: boundless love, compassion, sympathetic joy and equanimity. If this prayer is well understood, it really awakens one's Enlightened mind. It is important not to confuse equanimity with lack of caring, however. As Buddhists, we know that mind is inherently positive, that

The Bodhisattva Vow

Jang chhub nying por chhi kyi bar
Sang gye nam la kyab su chhi
Chho dang jang chhub sem pa yi
Tshog la ang de zhin kyab su chhi
Ji tar ngon gyi de sheg kyi
Jang chhub thug ni kye pa dang
Jang chhub sem pai lab pa la
De dag rim zhin ne pa tar
De zhin dro la phen don du
Jang chuub sem ni kye gyi zhing
De zhin du ni lab pa la ang
Rim pa zhin du lab par gyi

Until I reach the heart of enlightenment,
I take refuge in all the Buddhas,
and similarly in the Dharma and the assembly of
    Bodhisattvas.
Just as the Tathagatas of the past
generated the enlightened attitude and were trained as
    Bodhisattvas
and gradually came to dwell in the ten Bodhisattva
    stages,
likewise, for the sake of all sentient beings,
I, too, will engender the enlightened attitude,
and will follow the training stage by stage,
and gradually, as they did, become proficient.

equanimity is something warm and encompassing which appears when the mind rests in itself, as an expression of its perfect nature. Mind is never something neutral, sinful in basis or dangerously incomplete; its essence is timeless perfection itself.

With the last sentence of the text, the whole Refuge-tree dissolves into light, which then streams into us like water mixing with water, and we become inseparably one. There are several ways to do this, but the following two are used the most: (1) we dissolve the Refuge-tree opposite to the way we built it up. This means letting the Protectors dissolve into the Bodhisattvas, the Bodhisattvas into the books, these into the Buddhas, these into the Yidams, and the Yidams into the Karmapa. Then all the Lamas melt into the Karmapa who becomes rainbow light and streams into our heart. Or (2), everything melts into the Karmapa at the same time, who then enters our heart.

The time we spend resting in this stage is what changes prostrations from the gymnastics of an inchworm into the main path to Mahamudra. Here, we ourselves become the Refuge. We become limitless, beyond hope and fear. Mind rests in itself and there is nothing to be obtained.

Afterwards, out in the world, we strengthen our oneness with the Refuge whenever possible and try to experience our surroundings as the Pure Land, seeing things on the highest possible level. We return to the prostrations whenever we can, keeping view and practice in balance. The text should be read frequently in English, in order to really understand what we're doing, and from time to time in Tibetan, to pick up the centuries of good energies accumulated in that language.

The six lines which accompany the prostrations should always be repeated in Tibetan. We read the text before and after the practice, while sitting, and it is generally said that "the cushion should stay warm." This means that if we have to go to the bathroom or pick up the phone for a moment, we don't need to begin again because we are still in the stream of what's happening. If we do several distinct sessions during the day, however, we should read the text through each time.

There are a number of methods for counting. The most popular in the West uses a mala with 27 beads which fits on our hand. Each time we stand up between prostrations, we move on to the next bead. Four times around is equivalent to a large mala of 108 beads. Like many Tibetans, one can also use either stones or coins which are pushed right and left. The latest tools being used are the small, hand-held devices for counting traffic. Technical innovations are welcome until someone appears with a prostration-board which moves up and down by itself.

Quality is important—the surface on which we slide, the cushions for knees and stomach, and the gloves, socks or tissues which protect our hands. All should function well. One question that's often asked is why we count the prostrations, that this makes a devotional practice too mechanical. The reason for counting is that it makes everything more goal-oriented so that we do more. We Westerners often think that numbers are not spiritual, but in the Ngondro, they are an important protection against fooling ourselves.

These prostrations work especially to purify the body and build up merit. The next practice, Dorje Sempa, also purifies speech and mind.

CHAPTER TWO

Dorje Sempa   *? Dorje Orgyen ? Chary ?*

THE SECOND OF THE PRELIMINARIES, the 100-syllable mantra of Dorje Sempa (Skt., Vajrasattva), is also tantric, meaning that it works with our totality. This may be surprising since, in this practice, we are "only" sitting. But concentration on a Buddha form and on the nectar brings about a very deep change in our body, while mantras and the identification with Enlightenment transform our speech and mind.

Whatever happens to us is a product of our karma. Actions in former lives lead us to a particular genetic makeup, to our deepest traits of character, and to birth in a specific place. In order to help us remove the negativity which hasn't yet ripened, all Buddhas unite their purifying power in the form of Dorje Sempa. In this second part of the Ngondro, we are given a method for burning all poisonous seeds so that we shall no longer be hampered by negativity, and the meditation is very effective. We can really expect more space in our mind, less obstacles, and a clearer view which enables us to do more for others.

Dorje Sempa is where the love and insight of space reach us in ways which purify the deepest levels of our mind. He dissolves what would otherwise bring suffering in this life, after death, or in future lives, making all situations conducive to maturity and growth. In the three lower Tantra classes, where the energy fields—or mandalas—focus on the potential or wisdom of Enlightenment, the central Buddha is usually Vairocana, but in the highest Tantra class, which emphasizes the energy and spontaneity of Enlightenment, Dorje Sempa often occupies this position and is difficult to distinguish from Dorje Chang.

The name Dorje Sempa means "the Diamond Mind," and this aspect of Enlightenment may emanate out of an all-good space in families of five or a hundred, white or in the five wisdom-colors. It may appear as a single form, in union, as an expression of great joy as Demchok, or powerfully protective as Dorje Phurba (Skt., Vajra Kilaya). I don't know any other aspect that can be realized through so many different meditations, all ultimately changing everything into Ogmin, the Pure Land of "No Down." In the Ngondro, however, since the aim is deep purification, we meditate on the single, peaceful aspect and emphasize the developing phase of holding him above us and repeating the mantra. Therefore, the dissolving phase of identifying and becoming one with him is kept short.

Actually, meditating on the various forms is like entering the same house through different doors. The essence of any of the meditations is to transform hate, anger and ill will into mirror-like wisdom. Dorje Sempa is the activity of the Buddha Akshobhya and, among the five Buddha families, this is the type of insight he expresses. Hate and anger are the most harmful feelings that can arise, the worst enemies of all. Desires can be satisfied, at least for periods of time, while hate and anger give a negative view of the whole world, causing harmful conditions to come together which bring about paranoia, accidents, diseases like cancer, and so on. At or after death, these feelings re-emerge as the experience of unbearable heat or cold (the hell realms) and cause outer and inner suffering also when we become human again. The most important work, therefore, is to remove them totally, to transform them into that completely clear, mirror-like state which this practice makes possible.

While repeating the 100-syllable mantra of Dorje Sempa, a strange zoological garden of unwanted impressions may come up. These are caused by previous actions, some long forgotten and some going back to former lives. We should welcome them; no matter how outlandish they may be, we can be sure of one thing: whatever we experience is on its way out, not on its way in. We are seeing the backs, not the faces of the animals. As we begin to understand that these mixed experiences will lighten the mind, we can even start feeling good about them. It's like a useless party when the impossible guests are finally going home. One feels relieved when saying good-bye.

We may also have more direct and positive signs: the pleasant feeling of walking on air may occur and gradually become constant; the universe will seem to have less suffering, stickiness and narrowness, and things become meaningful and radiant just because they are there. One may have dreams of wrestling with black giants or drinking milk and throwing up ink, etc.

Whatever it is, we should be glad. Something good is happening in our mind. Though our budding understanding of emptiness shows us that conditioned experiences are nothing but dreams, still, aspects of the good feelings which begin to arise: fearlessness, joy, and warmth, express the timeless nature of the mind itself. The more its veils fall away, the stronger these experiences become. They prove to be richer and more wonderful than anything we can imagine, and because it's the knots and hindrances in our present karmic condition which need to be removed, we consciously do this meditation, not as forms of energy and light, but in our present karmic body, with all its habits and weaknesses.

As mentioned earlier, this practice touches our totality. The 100 syllables of the mantra evoke 100 purifying Buddha aspects, both within our body and in the space around us. Our concentration on Dorje Sempa's form and on the white nectar which streams through us work to change the feeling of our body. The inner channels transmit more insight, and new levels of consciousness are experienced. We really get rid of lots of dead weight. As in all the powerful Diamond Way meditations, there is both a developing and a dissolving phase, each with its own deep and transformative psychological effects.

To keep our experience fresh, it is wise to alternate between singing the formal text in Tibetan and reading—or remembering—the steps of the meditation in our own language. Sometimes we should also do the more deliberate developing phases of the meditation, mentioned below, as an added richness.

After the Four Thoughts, Refuge and the wish to reach Enlightenment for the good of all beings, we become conscious of ourselves in our present form, in this body. Above our head, there condenses out of space an open, clear, white lotus flower. If we feel more at home with a water lily, that's also fine. Both are examples of practical purity because they get their nourishment from the mud, grow up through the water, and only in the (hopefully) pure air do they open up in their full beauty. Thus, they show how any disturbed feeling or state is really the raw material for Enlightenment.

After the experience of the flower has solidified, the mind's luminous intelligence now manifests in the form of a moon disc lying inside the flower, and this should be as radiant as possible. In Tibet, the full moon shines strongly. The country has no air-pollution and at altitudes of 13,000 feet or more, one can see almost as clearly at night as during the day. On top of this moon disc, there now appears the radiant, energy form of Dorje Sempa, beautiful, crystal clear and transparent.

His right hand holds a golden dorje vertically to his heart and the left hand holds a silver bell at his hip, with the mouth pointing upwards. His head is at a slight angle with a fine smile. He wears the ornaments of the Bodhisattvas, representing the joy and perfection of Enlightenment, and the jewels around his forehead express the five Buddha wisdoms. His short and long necklaces activate enlightened energies at different places in the body and his earrings symbolize patience. His hair is yogi style, with one third in a knot on his crown, while the rest falls freely over his shoulders. With a skirt of five-colored silks, showing his Tantric power, he sits, not in the full lotus of deep absorption, but with his right foot stretched over the lotus and down towards us. He faces in the same direction as we.

This is the short, daily version. Here are some suggestions from the commentaries on how we can enter the meditation in a more gradual and extended way: From the Tibetan letter Pam, the lotus appears. Inside this, manifests the letter Ah which transforms into the moon disc. In its center stands a white Hung which immediately becomes a standing Dorje with a Hung in the center. From this appears the radiant form of Dorje Sempa.

 PAM   AH   HUNG

If we have total confidence that Dorje Sempa is the essence of space itself and that he is there the moment we think of him, if we can hold the awareness of being one with him between the sessions of meditation, it is possible to let him appear directly before saying the Mantra. In most cases, however, the first approach will be most natural.

Then light streams out from Dorje Sempa to the countless Buddhas and Bodhisattvas in space and, when touched by the rays, they are instantaneously transformed into Dorje Sempas themselves. Big like mountains and small like dust, from all directions they fall into the Dorje Sempa above our heads and merge with him. He is now the purifying essence of all the Buddhas.

Next, we make strong wishes for purification. The text is especially suited for those who have already taken initiations, as recitation purifies all those subtle damaged vows of which most are not even aware. One should keep the intensity of the feeling, and make the wishes in such a way that they are relevant to our own situation, seeing them on outer, inner and secret levels. Or, we can simply think of all the beings we have harmed during all our lives and wish them everything good.

As Dorje Sempa feels the power of our wishes, he
smiles, and, centrally in his chest at the level of his heart,
there now appears a very fine, flat moon disc lying down. In
the center stands a white letter Hung, as fine as if painted
with a single hair. The smaller we can imagine this, the
stronger our concentration will be.

It's useful to keep in mind that Dorje Sempa's body is
transparent like a crystal and that everything is seen
through the clarity of our mind, rather than through our
eyes. The term "visualization" is a misleading expression
for this kind of awareness which, in many people, works
without visual images. Actually, "know" would be a better
word for the many intelligent people whose minds
understand things directly or through abstraction but do
not produce pictures. The important thing is to know that
the Buddhas are there whenever we open up to them.

Around the letter Hung, written counterclockwise in
this practice and standing, is the 100-syllable-mantra which
we imagine either as a ring of light or, more dynamically, as
an open spiral of light which winds out two and a half times
from the Hung in the center towards the rim of the moon
disc. The closed circle is taught by Kalu Rinpoche, the spiral
by Karmapa. Both are good, but here we are instructed by
the lamas to perform the practice with the mantra standing
still.

When we begin to repeat the mantra, Dorje Sempa's
limitless love is activated. From the letter Hung and the
moon disc, centrally in his heart, white nectar arises
continuously and flows in all directions until it fills him
completely. Now, from the big toe of his right foot

Dorje Sempa

stretched down towards us, a powerful stream of purifying white nectar shoots out. It pushes through the opening in the crown of our head and, at the same time, flows through and over our body. From the top on down we are filled ever more with nectar, powerfully like an enormous waterfall, and deeply like a quietly flowing river.

DORJE SEMPA'S HUNDRED SYLLABLE MANTRA

Om Benza Sato Samaya/ Manupalaya/ Benza Sato Tenopa/ Tita Dri Do Me Bhawa/ Suto Kayo Me Bhawa/ Supo Kayo Me Bhawa/ Anurakto Me Bhawa/ Sarwa Siddhi Memtrayatsa/ Sarwa Karma Sutsa Me/ Tsitam Shriya Kuru Hung/ Ha Ha Ha Ha Ho Bhagawan/ Sarwa Tathagata/ Benza Ma Me Muntsa Benzi Bhawa Maha Samaya Sato Ah

SHORT MANTRA: Om Benza Sato Hung

---

prov/
same
mantra
?

We should experience the purification in the way that feels most natural. Both the traditional and more "modern" associations are fine at this point. For example, we may feel like we are in a car wash, or think of acids and other chemicals cleaning us out, not only the gentle nectar. All the harmful things we have ever done, thought or said are now pressed out of us like ink, soot and smoke. From the pores of our skin, our anus, and the soles of our feet, everything dark and gooey is pushed out and washed away by the nectar flowing over us. Latent diseases leave like pus and blood. Confused and neurotic thought patterns disappear, looking like strange insects and deep water fish. We may imagine harmful words dissolving in our throat, and disturbing impressions falling like pieces of coal, directly from our heart. All the time, the purifying nectar continues streaming through and over us.

Underneath us the earth opens and all the negativity, which would have matured later as suffering, now streams in there, leaving us ever more radiant and pure. People who feel that their disturbances have outer causes can imagine these as demons sitting underneath, greedily gobbling up both negativity and nectar, then walking away happily. Now, the whole debt has been paid and the connection is dissolved, leaving them with the blessing of the nectar. Whoever experiences negativity as an inner process should simply let everything stream into the ground and disappear in emptiness.

While repeating the 100-syllable mantra, we shift our focus but stay inside the totality of the experience. Sometimes we are conscious of Dorje Sempa's form. Then we shift to his loving face with the fine smile, to his golden dorje and silver bell, or to the moon disc or the mantra composed around the letter Hung. Then we experience the nectar flowing through us and stay with the bodily sensations evoked. From time to time, we are aware of the earth underneath us where everything disappears.

Four "powers" increase purification and are good companions on our way. First, the understanding that we have not yet reached Enlightenment due to earlier negativity. Next, the wish to purify through the effective use of meditation and mantra. Third, the decision not to do harmful acts again. And fourth, the intent and effort to act in a positive manner. These four powers may be explained differently, but all follow the same progression.

When we've said as many of the long mantras as we can, we are purified. The earth closes and our bodies are now tight. The mantra still stands in Dorje Sempa's heart above us, and we start the short mantra, "OM BENZA SATO HUNG," while the nectar fills us up, the way a crystal is filled with milk. Repeating the short mantra until the nectar from the crown of our head touches his foot—at least one mala around—we ask strongly for assurance that the purification was complete. With a loving smile, Dorje Sempa answers: "Dear daughters and sons of the good Mahayana family, everything harmful from you and all living beings is now totally purified; I promise you that." He then dissolves into light, which streams down into us, and we become inseparably one.

There are many ways to do the meditation, but we use the simplest. The focus is on purifying ourselves and developing the confidence that this has really occurred. Later on, if we are given Dorje Sempa as a Yidam, we can then enjoy the richness of complicated and fascinating phases which are possible in this meditation.

The important thing is always to *be* him as well as we can; to see everything as his Pure Land, and all beings as Dorje Sempas in the five wisdom colors, to hear all sounds as his mantra, and experience all thoughts as his spontaneous wisdom. In that way, enlightenment is only natural. We should keep this awareness as well as we can between our periods of practice.

This second part of the Ngondro, the 111,111

repetitions of the 100-syllable mantra, may take a well-trained person longer than the prostrations. Saying the mantra very quickly gives intensity, but spending less than a quarter hour on one mala around diminishes the benefit.

 We musn't lose a single syllable, as each of them activates a Buddha family.

Finally, a few words about practice. The goal is always the spontaneous, effortless state of awareness, and the quickest way to get there is by identifying with perfection. Either going the direct way of simply being fearless, spontaneously joyful, and actively compassionate, or the indirect one of meditating on forms which clearly are so, nothing works better. The essential thing in such "visualizations" is that the mind "knows" what it's opening up to. For example, I may ask you what the house of your parents looked like and you will know; you will have a feeling of it whether there is a visual image or not. It's this knowingness which gives the experience. Everyone can dream. No one has a "blind" mind. So, be confident in the richness of space. Understand that Enlightenment is there whenever we even think of it. Devotion to our Lama and Refuge are all that we need, for without confidence and devotion, there is no Diamond Way.

CHAPTER 3

The Mandala Offerings

5 Buddha families ?

A FEW PHYSICAL OBJECTS are needed for this practice which builds up both positive impressions (merit) and awareness. We need polished white rice, if possible long grain (which lasts better than the short round variety), and it is a good idea to color some red, blue, yellow and green as an offering to the five Buddha families. Also, small semi-precious *?* stones, beads and things like that give the rice a precious feeling.

If we make the offerings as pleasant as we can, the joy and benefit of the practice will be greatly enhanced. We already know the rich feeling of something sliding through our hands from the beach, when we played with sand, and probably retain it also from former lives as gold diggers or farmers, sticking our open hands into precious dust or different kinds of grain.

As some rice will get lost every day, we'll be adding more. Therefore, it's wise to prepare far more than our initial need. Purity is essential in this practice. When Hannah and I did it in the Himalayas in 1971, people tied a cloth around their mouths so that no breath could touch the offerings. It probably doesn't feel so natural in the West, with our good dental care, but whoever eats garlic, onions or strong cheese should brush their teeth before starting.

During the meditation, whatever falls outside the cloth into our lap is not used again. Instead, we add new rice. The old grains hold the blessing, while the new add freshness.

Two mandalas are needed. The more precious—or larger—of the two (for example, a silver plate) can be used for the mandala representing the Refuge, the so-called Drupay mandala. According to Lamini Karma Pema Wangchuk (better known as Hannah Nydahl), the Drupay mandala is placed on the altar, in front of the place where we do the practice. If we don't have a Drupay mandala, we can hold the Refuge in our mind instead, although the more objects we actually have in front of us, the fewer we need to imagine. On the second, rounded disc—the Chöpay mandala (usually made of copper or brass)—the offerings themselves will be made.

This Chöpay mandala should not be too large or heavy, since we hold both this and the mala in our left hand during the entire session. We generally use a convex mandala disc about 15 cm/6 in. in diameter, with a rim about 3-4 cm/1-1/2 in. wide. Most of these come from the Indian Himalayas or Nepal, and you can get them in the Dharma shops of different centers or from friends who have already finished their mandalas.

"Offering up" means offering to someone. It has a goal, full Enlightenment, and for that reason we first build up the Drupay mandala, the mandala of attainment. We

Mandala Offerings

begin by placing a handful of rice on the cloth in our lap and
then we symbolically purify the mandala: we cleanse the
plate with the inner side of the right wrist going around
three times in a clockwise direction and once counterclockwise. While doing this, we repeat two mantras in
Sanskrit: OM BENZA AMRITA HUNG PAY, and OM SOBHAWA
SHUDDHA SARWA DHARMA SOBHAWA SHUDDO HANG,
which purifies everything with nectar, then dissolves it into
space.

We then meditate that, out of space, the mandala
appears as a magnificent rainbow palace in the sky in front,
and then we place five heaps of rice on the disc, one in the
middle and one in each of the four directions. We may also

use tormas or biscuits. The one in the center represents the Lama, the one in front of us, the Yidams, the left one, the Buddhas, the one behind, the Teachings, and the right one, the Bodhisattvas and practicing ones. Here the place for the Protectors is unlimited, the whole Refuge is resting on a living cloud of them.

We understand that space and truth are one, and through the three centers of forehead, throat and heart, as in the Karmapa meditation, we send light to all Enlightened beings, asking them to melt into the rice heaps. Then we place this mandala on our altar or on a high place in front of us. If the practice flows well, we can let it stay there until we have finished the 111,111 repetitions, but if we stop for a longer period, we have to build up the mandala once again. We now hold this Refuge vividly before us, while offering again and again all that brings joy in the relative world. It is meaningless to give to Enlightenment something already Enlightened, or to offer what belongs to the three lower levels of existence.

For daily practice, we take the second disc, the Chöpay mandala, in our left hand, cleaning its surface with our right wrist, at the beginning of each session. We go three times clockwise and once counterclockwise, then clockwise again, this time reciting the 100-syllable Dorje Sempa mantra three times. We think that all outer and inner impurities and veils are now removed from ourselves and all beings. Then we say "OM BENZA BHUMI AH HUNG" and spray some perfumed oil or water on the disc. This is the dew of Enlightenment fertilizing basic consciousness.

Due to the karma of each being and what would help the most, the Buddha taught several ways of seeing the universe. Here, we use the one in the Abhidharma. As the goal is the Mahamudra state, however, beyond all concepts, the methods employed are secondary. What matters are the seeds we plant in our mind. The disc represents the primordial mind, the golden base of all things, and we should see this on the highest level possible, covered by a limitless ocean and enlivened by the wind.

We then take a bit of rice in our right hand and, reciting the mantra "OM BENZA RAY KAY AH HUNG," we make a counterclockwise circle of grain around the rim of the mandala disc. This is the iron wall, the magnetic field, which holds the universe together. After this, we come to the 37 signs of a perfect universe, the way it's experienced by desire-gods. While slowly reciting the text, we place 37 heaps of rice on the disc. Many of you have already seen how a mandala like this is offered before higher initiations. Only there, three additional rings are often used, tapering upwards towards a jewel and making the three-dimensional quality more clear. In the Ngondro practice, we only use the base disc, leaving more to the mind.

The effects of the offerings go much deeper than the conditioned values of changing cultures. They touch timeless experiences of body and mind. Desires are satisfied which people have at all times and places, and our deepest capacity for psychological richness is activated. Constantly offering expressions of timeless perfection is just as meaningful today as it has always been. If we can trust this and are not disturbed by the more exotic culturally determined aspects of the practice, it will be effective on all levels.

And so, out of space, a world system appears in the

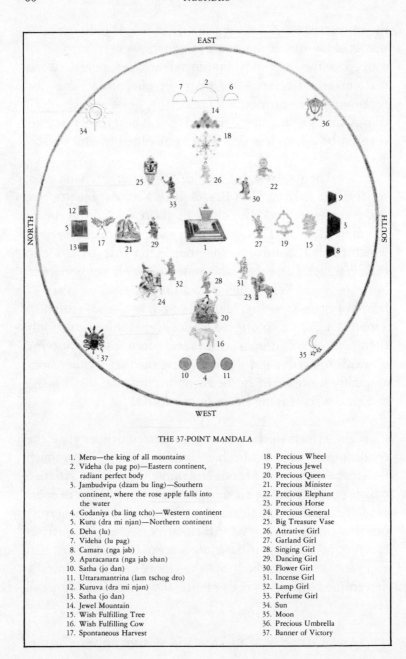

THE 37-POINT MANDALA

1. Meru—the king of all mountains
2. Videha (lu pag po)—Eastern continent, radiant perfect body
3. Jambudvipa (dzam bu ling)—Southern continent, where the rose apple falls into the water
4. Godaniya (ba ling tcho)—Western continent
5. Kuru (dra mi njan)—Northern continent
6. Deha (lu)
7. Videha (lu pag)
8. Camara (nga jab)
9. Aparacanara (nga jab shan)
10. Satha (jo dan)
11. Uttaramantrina (lam tschog dro)
12. Kuruva (dra mi njan)
13. Satha (jo dan)
14. Jewel Mountain
15. Wish Fulfilling Tree
16. Wish Fulfilling Cow
17. Spontaneous Harvest

18. Precious Wheel
19. Precious Jewel
20. Precious Queen
21. Precious Minister
22. Precious Elephant
23. Precious Horse
24. Precious General
25. Big Treasure Vase
26. Attrative Girl
27. Garland Girl
28. Singing Girl
29. Dancing Girl
30. Flower Girl
31. Incense Girl
32. Lamp Girl
33. Perfume Girl
34. Sun
35. Moon
36. Precious Umbrella
37. Banner of Victory

form of a discus, thick in the middle and getting thinner toward the rim. In its center stands Meru or Rirab, the mountain where gods and demigods live. Near the outer edge of the disc are the four "main" and eight "sub"-continents containing intelligent life, where beings with human-like karmas are reborn. Thus, although everything appears freely in space—and may actually be representations of galaxies—in order to relate it to our daily experience, we imagine a solid base and magnetic mountains which keep everything together. Between the central mountain and the rim are seven square mountain chains and seven seas which fill the space between them.

The first rice heap which we put in the middle of the disc represents Mount Meru. Here from the top and down, live those beings who experience the three god realms: the formless or abstract realm, although still with the illusion of an "I," the form states where one experiences complete aesthetic beauty, and the states where wishes and desires are spontaneously fulfilled, but new ones constantly arise.

At the base of the mountain live the demigods, who are constantly fighting and jealous both of each other and of the gods. The four sides of the mountain consist of precious stones in four colors: the east is white, and of crystal; the south, blue and of lapis; the west, red and of ruby; and the north is green and made of emerald. They send their colored lights out which are reflected by the sky and the seven seas between the continents.

Next, we build up the four main continents in the four cardinal directions. East in this system is the point furthest from us, meaning our north. It is white and shaped like a semicircle. The south is blue and shaped like a trapezoid.

The west is red and circular, and the north is green and square. The rice heaps will be placed in that order. It is said that the faces of the beings who live on these continents have the same shapes as the continents themselves.

One can imagine it like this. Here is our world which is the southern continent, Jambuling. On the other side of the Milky Way is the northern continent, etc. On three of the four continents, there are fixed lifespans. On one, people live for 250 years, on the next for 500, and on the third, until they are 1,000 years old. Also, the size of the people varies proportionally from place to place. The longer they live, the larger they are. These worlds are rather like gods' worlds.

Our world is the one where the lifespan is variable. It's also the place where the most disturbing feelings are, as well as where the Buddhas manifest. Our world has the most raw material to work with, while the more godly states, as well as the god worlds themselves, provide little opportunity for Enlightened ones to work. There is too little emotional intensity where beings enjoy their happy states but don't do much else. In the *Tibetan Book of the Dead*, we are advised not to take rebirth there because there's no possibility for development.

Now the eight sub-continents are offered up, and the colors, forms and everything else are like the main continents, only much smaller and positioned to the right and left of them. When we place the rice heaps on the disc, we cross our hands over, putting first a pile to the right and then one to the left of the main continent. As we place the rice heaps in order on the disc, we are offering our concentration on this ideal world system to the Refuge in front.

The names of the countries in the text are in Tibetan, their respective translation in Sanskrit. Their meaning is the same and they explain the different qualities of these countries. For instance, Shar-Lu Pag Po, means "East: noble body."

The next round of offerings is made more towards the center of the mandala, and the movement from now on goes in concentric circles ever closer to Mount Meru. We first offer what is especially valuable in these other worlds: in the East, the jewel mountain, in the South, the wish-fulfilling tree, in the West, "a cow which may be milked as much as wished," and in the North, the harvest which appears without cultivation. All are things which give a feeling of richness. One can wish for whatever one wants. Everything is there.

The next points of the four main directions are the special possessions of a Chakravartin, a world monarch. Through the power of his good karma, certain things are simply there. He owns a precious wheel with a thousand spokes, the symbol of his universal power, and a wish-fulfilling jewel. His consort is a wonderful, precious queen who has all the marks of feminine perfection. He also has a wise minister who fulfills his wishes even before he has recognized them himself. We let them all arise in our mind while placing the rice heaps in the proper order.

For the next round, this time putting rice on the intermediate points, there is a precious elephant in the Southeast which perseveres and never gets fatigued. In the Southwest is a precious horse of incredible speed. In the Northwest, there is a brave general who conquers all enemies, and in the Northeast, a huge precious vase. It contains an inexhaustible supply of jewels and treasure.

Further towards the center, in the four cardinal directions, come the first four of eight wonderful offering girls: the graceful one who smiles charmingly, the flower garland girl, and the girls of song and dance. We then let the next four appear and offer up in the intermediate directions: the flower, incense, lamp-carrying and perfumed water girls. They offer great joy to the senses.

Finally, from the inner ring we again go to the rim of the mandala disc for four points which are positioned above the others, and we offer them in a diagonal fashion. In the Northeast, we offer the sun; in the Southwest, the moon; in the Southeast, the precious umbrella, which means the conquering of all suffering; and in the Northwest, the perfect banner of victory.

Several of these objects are precious because the Buddha blessed them. In very traditional Indo-Tibetan culture, they are seen to be beautiful and desirable, and they can still touch us directly even today.

I found that out myself, ten years after Hannah and I had finished this practice. In 1981, in Sikkim, on the night H. H. the 16th Karmapa died, I had an intense dream where the old symbols reappeared in a modern setting. First, I flew in a helicopter and, looking up towards the propeller, I saw that it was the precious Dharma wheel. Then I walked forward on the crown of a gigantic Karmapa statue. Near the forehead, there were two big boxes. I opened them, found thick packages of dollar-bills and jewels and threw them into the air for the good of all beings. That was Norbu

Rinpoche, the precious, wish-fulfilling gem. Suddenly, the Danish Queen Margaret appeared in a sports sweater and I took her to my chest and asked her what she was doing in my dream. Then came the precious elephant, in the form of a big BMW car and the precious horse, in the form of a BMW motorcycle. Their meaning was exactly the same, perseverance and speed. Finally, after many other things which now slip my mind, I stood in an enormous field of dry, grey-brown earth when an enormous wave came from the right, flooded the field and then receded again leaving behind ripe grain, standing very tall. This was the spontaneous harvest.

Actually, during that night, I had been given the signs of a world conqueror, a universal monarch. And, I now think differently of the mandala symbols which my critical Western mind couldn't take too seriously before.

We read the root text, sometimes in Tibetan and sometimes in English, trying to maintain awareness of it all while point by point building up a universe containing the 37 precious offerings. The very best and purest of gods and men are now there, and we pray to the Refuge in front to accept this offering out of their compassion. Then we pray for blessing, holding the disc quite high in front of us and really offering it to the Refuge. I advise holding the mandala high; it evokes a strong, good feeling, but we only do that with the great mandalas, not with the small ones which we count.

Then, following the text, we repeat the names of those to whom we offer all this and the number of times we do it. Here, we need advanced mathematics, with numbers in the billions and hundreds of billions. It may all sound unspiritual, solid and materialistic, but the idea is that at some point, quantity becomes quality, and that our level of experience changes, simply through the great number of good impressions stored in the mind.

Good actions create pleasant experiences, the way bad actions bring suffering. But good impressions do more than that. They also give our mind the confidence to rest in its true nature and, thus, to experience its Enlightened qualities beyond any doubt or limitation. Results are the opposite when we bring others harm; after a while, we find ourselves in states where the bad effects cannot be controlled anymore, where we become paranoid or have real difficulties with the outer world.

Enormous surplus creates a new dimension of richness; one level of experience stops and another begins. A really rich man doesn't just have more money than a poor one, his mind also works differently. He is beyond many of the things which limit the life of a poor man. Likewise for the spiritually rich, things happening are a play, while for narrower minds, they are bitter truth, and deadly serious.

Next, we again ask the Buddhas for blessing. We keep the whole mandala with the 37 offerings in our left hand, take some rice in our right, and throw it, as our offering, to the Refuge in front of us. While doing this, we say, "OM MANDALA PUTSA MEGA SAMUDRA SAPARANA SAMAYE AH HUNG," and wipe the rice away with the inner side of our wrist so that it falls on the cloth in our lap. So, neither during the great nor the small mandala offerings do we just tilt the disc to clear it. Instead, we use our wrist each time.

When Hannah and I did this practice, the 37 points

were repeated after 108 of the small offerings, that is, after
every mala around. Since then, it has become simpler. Now,
we usually just offer the great mandala at the beginning and
end of each sitting.

Then we continue with the text, praying that all
hindrances along the way be removed and that we be able to
fulfill the wishes of all Buddhas from past, present and
future; that we will neither waste time as ordinary,
confused beings in the conditioned world, nor be satisfied
with our own liberation in the Nirvana of simple peace.
Samsara is the condition where the mind is constantly
running after its experiences, blinded by attachment and
aversion, and stuck in conditioned existence, the best
moments of which have far less intensity than the timeless
experience of Enlightenment, while the "small" Nirvana
mentioned here means cutting oneself off from the world.
On the one hand, one cannot be harmed, but on the other,
one cannot do much for others and it is not productive.

What we want to attain is the highest Nirvana, the
perfect and truly exciting one. Here, there is neither
attachment to conditioned existence nor to a state of peace;
both are the mind's richness. If nothing is there, that is the
mind's space, intuition, and potential. When something
appears, it is seen as the clarity and free play of the mind
without expectation or fear. This non-sticky, non-gluey
Nirvana is our goal, and we pray that all beings may reach
it.

Now we have arrived at the four lines and 33 syllables
which we repeat 111,111 times during the offerings. It is a
short form of the great mandala, leaving more to our
imagination. Here we offer 7 piles of rice representing the

Meru mountain, the four continents, the sun and the moon, wipe the rice off and build another perfect world which we also give away. Being rich beyond measure, we don't need to take anything home. The Tibetan syllables we repeat while doing this mean, "The ground is sprinkled with scented water, strewn with flowers and adorned with Mount Meru, the four continents, the sun and the moon. I imagine this to be a Buddhafield. Through making such an offering may all beings abide in the Pure Lands." The more precious the things we can pass on the better. Time with close friends, exciting love, high speed, heaps of jewels and light, views over mountains when the snow is crisp and reflects the sun, or the wonderful hours spent in a Silver Solarium! We let arise what is possible from our own inner richness and then simply pass it on. As the weeks of doing this practice add up, our whole life becomes an offering of joy.

When we have done as many small offerings as we can during a session, we repeat the 37 point mandala and the text following that, until once again we have arrived at the small mandala. We then read on from there, making the outer, inner, secret and absolute offerings to our Lamas. The outer offerings are different kinds of tormas or offering-cakes. The inner ones are nectar. The secret ones are the joys of sexual union and the absolute offering is space itself, the openness from which everything arises. We offer these and all universes, and here, we shouldn't think that we are giving something which doesn't belong to us. We are not apart from the totality of all things and so, naturally, we can offer up everything good. We pray to the Buddhas to give us the most perfect abilities, especially that of Mahamudra, the ultimate state, where seer, thing seen and seeing are one, and the mind rests beyond any disturbance whatsoever.

Our last wish is that Merit and Wisdom become perfected in all beings. Finally, the whole Refuge dissolves into us, and we become one taste: there is no longer any separation between the Refuge and ourselves. Enlightenment inside and outside unite, and there are no longer two. We stay in this limitless, radiant, joyful space as well as we can.

Finally, in order to do this quite complicated practice with assurance, we need the instruction of someone who has already done it and who can show us the proper movements involved.

CHAPTER FOUR

Guru Yoga

THE FOURTH AND LAST part of the Ngondro, the Guru Yoga, deals mainly with the accumulation of wisdom and with our integration into the Karma Kagyu transmission lineage and the absorption of its full blessing. The first two practices emphasized purification, and the third developed inner wealth, but all this occurred while staying in our habitual forms as beings of flesh and blood.

Here, we first let everything dissolve into emptiness. Reciting OM SOBHANA SHUDDHA SARWA DHARMA SOBHA-WA SHUDDO HANG, all phenomena are purified and disappear back into space. Our awareness then arises in the form of Dorje Phagmo, the red dakini, beautiful, transparent and naked. Standing on our left leg with the right pulled up, our left hand holds a skull-bowl at the level of our heart, filled with the nectar of wisdom, while our right hand holds the chopping knife at shoulder height, cutting off all narrow-mindedness. Being this radiant body of light, habits based on the limiting experiences of having a body cease and our receptivity to blessing is greatly enhanced.

Dorje Phagmo is one of the central yidams of the

Kagyupas and, being female, naked and red, she represents
the ultimate intuitive wisdom of space. It is best if you can
experience being her in every detail, but sufficient just to
have the confidence that you have now really become Dorje
Phagmo.

From the first sentence onwards, we recognize the
original Kagyupa text. We open ourselves to the root-Lama
Karmapa above us or to his form as Dorje Chang, knowing
that they are one. In our lineage, the Lama is the most
important aspect.

A thousand years ago, when Marpa visited Naropa for
the second time, to bring the Six Doctrines back to Tibet, a
huge blue, intensely radiating energy-field appeared at
Naropa's side. It was the Buddha Kye Dorje (Skt., Hevajra)
in union with Dagmema (Skt., Nairatmya), Marpa's yidam.
They sparkled like a thousand suns and next to them,
Naropa looked like any old Indian, not especially remark-
able. Naropa then asked, "Who do you want to greet first?"
Thinking, "I see Naropa every day, but this other one looks
special," Marpa first welcomed Hevajra. Naropa said,
"Mistake; in our lineage the Lama is always the most
important." He then dissolved the whole power-field into
light and drew it into his heart.

Whatever form we meditate on, whether Chenrezig,
Dorje Sempa, Dolma or Mahakala, all are different aspects
of the Karmapa. Even the various teachers of our lineage,
both Tibetans and Westerners, embody the activities of the
Karmapa (at least as long as they don't make any special
organizations of their own which cause confusion or directly harm people). We should not be regarded as individuals,
but rather as more or less open channels to him.

When we think of the Karmapa, we receive the blessing of the Black Crown as well, while the reason for using the blue energy-form of Dorje Chang is the difficulty some people have in seeing a human body as pure. For those who are able to do so, the leap to the realm where everything is fresh and radiant is very short. By gradually lifting our level of seeing things, enlightened powers arise naturally and hindrances on the way dissolve. We thus let all perfection, the whole Refuge appear above us in the radiant space of mind.

The insight that everything arises from the mind is a "must" if we want Enlightenment, and in the Guru Yoga we can work better with this understanding than before. While doing our prostrations, a Refuge Tree was still needed. The mind stuck to material things and even during mandala offerings, we still had the physical support of the five heaps of rice. In the Guru Yoga, however, Karmapa is above our heads, and the whole Refuge is in rows above and around him. The holders of the transmission lineage form the central chain, the "Golden Chain of the Kagyu Transmission."

On the very top is Dorje Chang, followed by the Indian Mahasiddhas and then Marpa, Milarepa and Gampopa. Below them are all the Karmapas, Shamarpas, Situpas, Jamgon Kongtrul Rinpoches and Gyaltsap Rinpoches, down to the Karmapa directly above. If you have a teacher who is very close to you, who is faithful to the Karmapa and your source of essential teachings and blessings, you can imagine him either as being inseparable from the Karmapa or directly beneath him, as the Karmapa's activity.

While opening ourselves to this power-field, we think

and say: "Om: All-pervading one, you are the very nature of all things." (refer to Root text). How would we understand this today? Probably "space-information" is a meaningful term to use. Space is not something dead or separating; it is not some gap between us. On the contrary, space is alive with awareness and information. It contains, connects, transmits, and makes all things possible. Everything arises from space, is experienced by space, and returns to space again. Every intuitive insight, every spontaneous joy is a sign of this.

To H.H. the Karmapa, this all-seeing clairvoyance was his natural state. During the 12 years we were with him, he not only knew what everybody thought and felt, he often also said exactly what had happened or would happen both near and far. My books *Entering the Diamond Way* and the forthcoming *Riding the Tiger* tell about this. For example, when I had letters for him in the inside pocket of my jacket, he would point to them, knowing also who had written them, although I had forgotten all about them. He just knew this because he is not separated from anything. These things are possible only because space is truth and information, because Mind pervades and penetrates everything.

"Like space, you have neither abiding, coming nor going, nor any of the material characteristics of coming or going. Yet, like the moon reflecting in water, you manifest wherever someone thinks of you." (see Root text). It is really like that. No one can say where a thought or experience, a word or situation comes from. Whether we have the great good fortune to experience pure realms and meet female and male Buddhas, or just have ordinary experiences, they cannot be considered as having "come from anywhere." They arise from space itself and dissolve back into it again. Thoughts and emotions disappear within, while situations and worlds dissolve outside.

The purpose of all Diamond Way practices is to bring us certitude about the timeless nature of mind. When we are able to recognize mind as being ever-present and inseparable from space itself, we can dissolve into a rainbow, here and now. As this certainty becomes unshakeable, all hindrances and sorrows fall away on their own. If we are not completely sure, however, doubt is most convincingly dispelled by regular use of our Karmapa meditation. It permits us to really experience our oneness with him. Having the Karmapa arise in front of us, purifying and blessing us, we can most convincingly merge with his awareness-space.

Although truth is everywhere, our conditioned mind has difficulty receiving blessing without first having accomplished something. We feel more open when we also give something. That is one reason for the developing stages.

Opening up to the Refuge above will be easier if we first radiate light to all Buddhas and Bodhisattvas in space who then melt into the lineage. It suffices, however, to have the confidence that all the Buddhas are now spontaneously there, and it may shorten this phase considerably.

Here the Lama is also called "Glorious Heruka." Herukas are Buddhas in the state of Great Bliss from whose powerful bodies light and flames blaze in all directions. Mahakala is one; Dorje Phurba, Guru Drakpo, and Khorlo Demchog are others. All these manifestations of highest power are Herukas, expressions of male bliss which merge with female emptiness to spread ultimate Enlightenment.

"You who conquers the armies of negative forces" (see Root text). Here real deceptions and demons are referred to. They are not the wrathfully manifesting Buddhas who have an eye of wisdom on their foreheads, but rather beings of a very negative disposition. There is much literature about them, especially among the Tibetans.

Some demons formerly were people who practiced the developing stage of meditation very intensely, saying many Mantras and thereby accumulating great power. Neglecting the dissolving phase, however, where everything returns to emptiness and harmony develops, their meditation was without compassion, without thought for others. If much power and faulty motivation combine in this way, it is possible to be reborn as a demon.

"Gurus, Yidams, Dakinis and all those who accompany you—if now I pray to you with faith, please manifest here clearly through the power of your non-conceptual compassion" (see Root text). Here we invite the sources of blessing and inspiration, female as well as male, together with their retinue, trusting that they won't check our credentials but just be of help.

Many people think that friendship means hating what harms their friends, and of course there are many cases of a general nature where it would be cowardly not to make a stand, e.g., against suppression, brutality or distortion of the truth. Actually, however, we work most effectively for others when we can adapt to any arising situation, without disturbing emotions.

"I bow to my glorious sacred guru" (see Root text). Here we find again the seven-branch prayer. These seven steps make psychological sense, even though they should probably be translated into less dramatic language which more people can use.

Next, we make another set of wishes: "Bless me that I also gain that direct realization" (see Root text). And then come some passages which need special explanation: "Bless me that I may realize this illusory body to be the Nirmanakaya." This simply means that we will be able to use this body in an unsentimental way for the benefit of all beings. "Tulku" means illusory body, i.e. a body that is used as a tool.

There are four kinds of Buddha-activity. The peaceful, which brings people blessing and warmth; the augmenting, which arouses potential and gets things going everywhere; the inspiring/magnetizing, which awakens strong feelings of openness and love, and lastly, the powerful protective activity which gives security and takes rigorous action when necessary. Using our body in such ways, people around us will have maximum development.

"Bless me that I may realize the inner subtle energy-flows to be the Sambhogakaya." The breath of life refers to life-supporting winds pervading our body. Through Diamond-Way practice, these inner currents are increasingly experienced as ultimate bliss. Some of these energy-movements are experienced as extremely joyful even now, as when making love. Here, however, every bit of the body and every physical process is blissful all the time, and there is no coming down.

"Bless me that I may realize my mind to be the Dharmakaya." These three wishes reflect the ultimate level of insight and clearly show that this Chag-Chen-Ngondro leads to the full state of Mahamudra. Everything is there: using the body as a tool, experiencing inner winds and energy flows as highest bliss, and realizing the space-awareness of mind as deepest wisdom—what more do we want? The full meaning of Buddhism is concentrated in these three sentences that are placed so generously in our hands by the ninth Karmapa.

Having impressed our mind in this way, we call upon the huge power-field of the Mahamudra Lamas. It works through 43 lineage-holders (if we include the 16th Karmapa) and fully pervades space and time. Every moment and location contains truth as something spontaneous and unconditioned which may manifest outwardly as Buddhas, Bodhisattvas and their Pure Realms, or inwardly as deepest inspiration, bliss and courage. Though these states disappear when grasping at them, still they show what is timelessly true.

We often hear that ordinary awareness is a dream, but actually it has more relative reality than the dream state. A dream is experienced only by one's own mind, while daily consciousness is shared with others through common karmas and projections, through name and form. Daily awareness also includes the functions of body and speech. Keeping the non-attached wisdom of our dreams and using every power to do what is useful and what liberates beings, we transform ordinary awareness into enlightened activity.

This view guides our entry into the Mahamudra-transmission of the Kagyu-lineage and also into the Six Doctrines of Naropa. Both were combined and brought to Tibet by Marpa about a thousand years ago. Wisdom-lineages (Guru Rinpoche's Dzog-Chen and Marpa's Chag-Chen) were again united about 700 years ago by the third Karmapa, Rangjung Dorje, who gave us the Mahamudra prayer, and, since then, the paths of both energy and awareness are contained in the Kagyu lineage. The Enlightenment which follows from these energy-teachings was first taught by Buddha manifesting as Dorje Chang, and, after 1500 years of transmission through the Maha-siddhas in India, continued on through Tilopa, Naropa, Marpa, Milarepa, Gampopa and the Karmapas. The lineage invoked in this Ngondro, that of Mahamudra, also expressed itself first through Dorje Chang, but emphasizes the mind's awareness-space more than its clarity-energy.

The Refuge-trees we see are usually Mahamudra-trees and, therefore, Tilopa and Naropa can be seen in small bubbles of light on either side blessing everything. Lodro Rinchen, Saraha, Pagpa Ludrup (Nagarjuna), Shawaripa, Maitripa and Marpa, however, are centrally there, taking the positions below Dorje Chang. From Marpa and on, the Kagyu lineage has been the holder of the complete ways and means for realizing the mind.

And now we invoke them all by reading the text and try to understand what is said about each one. "Glorious Dorje Chang, who pervades all things . . . to you I pray" (see Root text). What is the real reason for all these prayers? Their purpose is neither to improve the activity of the Buddhas nor our position with them, but to open ourselves. Enlightenment cannot be made greater or smaller; it cannot be manipulated in this or that direction.

Rather, truth is wherever we think of it. The more we open ourselves, the more radiantly it appears everywhere, expressing all its Enlightened activities. Enlightenment is not passive: it is fearlessness, bliss and unconditional love. And, if we do our best, we can be sure that the Buddhas will save our lives, if necessary, and make them meaningful. The many prayers are thus given so that we can receive the blessing of the entire lineage.

This is also why we should be fully aware during the process of dying. By staying conscious, we won't miss those special opportunities for entering the Pure Land or Enlightenment which present themselves in abundance at the time of death and shortly thereafter.

The "natural state" referred to in the prayer is where the mind rests in its own fundamental nature, spontaneously and without effort. There are three levels of Mahamudra: The Base-Mahamudra, i.e., our Buddha-nature and confidence in it; the Path-Mahamudra, the mind resting in itself and learning from whatever happens; and the Fruit-Mahamudra, the experience of full Enlightenment. At first, this may all sound somewhat abstract, but just wait until the experience begins to grow inside you, picking up speed from everything encountered on the way.

"The Yidams, who bestow the two spiritual accomplishments, the multitude of Dharma-protectors . . . through the blessings of this prayer may the true nature, the Mahamudra as the ground, be realized." First we called in the blessing of the Lama, and now we open ourselves to the spontaneous insight transmitted by the Yidams, those fields of awareness and light which arise from Enlightenment and express its joy. They manifest as peaceful and wrathful, female and male, single or united, depending on what suits us. In this practice, we ourselves are the red Dorje Phagmo.

It is not necessary to always have the same Yidam. Though all have the same essence, different ones are more appropriate for various stages and accomplishments. They express the total inspiration and richness of the Buddha-mind; they are perfection in its highest form.

And what are the "two siddhis" mentioned? One involves great ability to play with the laws of nature which are our own collective karma, powers like those of Uri Geller. The other is really more important. It gives us the capability of helping beings on the deepest and innermost levels, removing their hindrances and disturbing habits and thereby creating the basis for growth. This is the truly meaningful achievement, but both are useful, and here we ask all Yidams to confer these powers upon us.

Then we turn to our Dharma-protectors, the masters of Buddha-activity working powerfully for the benefit of all. Here, most important are the omniscient Mahakalas, the female, male and united forces of enlightenment expressing protective power, the ones having the "Wisdom-eye." Very active also are the "Dam- Chens," those "held by their vows." They are not yet Bodhisattva-emanations but local and worldly energies which act close to the power fields of the Mahakalas. They are the ones who make trouble when we break our vows.

"Without conceiving of a goal, an achiever or an achievement . . . may the Mahamudra as the result become manifest." After the base and way, we now get the fruit.

There's no one going anywhere and there's nothing to get where we go; once again there's no expectation, no limitation, and nothing to imagine. Everything is spontaneous and effortless. When our train arrives at the station of our choice, we simply get off without thinking of what brought us there. We're simply aware in the moment and without a lot of fixed ideas. The mind has understood its potential, started moving and, after an organic, natural process, found itself at the goal. Now, all beings are male and female Buddhas, everything shines, is meaningful and completely right, and we recognize that it was actually like that all the time.

The prayers in the text so far have developed our devotion and liberating wisdom, letting all fixed ideas dissolve. Making entry into the Mahamudra level possible, they gradually lead to a full blossoming of our mind.

Then follows a lineage-prayer. "Great Dorje Chang, Tilopa, Naropa, Marpa, Milarepa, Prince of Dharma, Gampopa, Karmapa, who knows all past, present and future, the holders of the four great and the eight lesser lineages . . . I pray to you." Here again, we see that the lineage is what gives power to our wishes. We call on the Karmapa and, at the same time, we are conscious of the whole golden Transmission lineage of the Kagyus, above him in space.

Gampopa had both the Karmapa and three other main students who started so-called "great" transmission-lineages, meaning that they came directly from him. Today, they have been absorbed into the Karma Kamtsang and are carried on through the Karmapa and his lineage holders. Concerning the eight smaller lineages from Pamo Drupa, the Drigungs are important in Ladakh, and the Drugpas are the main holders of Buddhism in Bhutan. There is also one lineage which had nearly died out, called Shangpa Kagyu. It doesn't follow the transmission of Tilopa, Naropa, Marpa, Milarepa and so on, but comes through Niguma, the sister of Naropa. She developed a system which requires less physical strength, making it useful for women, and also, the visualizations are not so detailed. This lineage had nearly disappeared until Lodro Taye picked it up, and it didn't grow until Kalu Rinpoche came under the broad wings of the Karmapa. The Karmapa sent him to Bhutan in 1953 to organize for the exodus which was to come six years later, and after coming down from Tibet, he let Kalu Rinpoche carry on his transmission inside the Karma Kamtsang.

The incomparable protectors of beings, the Dhagpo Kagyus, are those descended from Gampopa or Dhagpo Lharje. Actually, people joke that there are two Kagyu transmissions, the Dhagpo Kagyus for the monks and the Marpa Kagyus for the Yogis and lay people. Since the 15th Karmapa, however, who had several wives and a dozen high incarnate children, it is clear that we don't need to make any such separation. We get the full transmission from both yogis and monks, though the emphasis in the teachings may be on a quicker versus a more gradual way.

"I will also uphold the tradition of the Kagyu lamas; grant your blessing that I may follow the example of their wondrous deeds." The power of the transmission is in its completeness and purity, and in the loyalty, power and unshakeability of teachers whose words and actions tally. It has nothing to do with ego-games, with personal likes or dislikes, or with the charm or lack of charm of the Guru.

"Weariness with Samsara is taught to be the foot of meditation . . . that he may be unattached to success and honor." These are fundamental things one has to check from time to time. Between the absolute renunciation of Milarepa and the attachments of ordinary beings, we have a yardstick by which we can measure our own motivation. "Devotion is taught to be the head of meditation . . . that uncontrived devotion may arise in him." So non-attachment is the foot, while devotion united with a readiness to learn is the head of meditation.

If we don't think the Lama has much to give, we might as well go somewhere else. If we feel a connection, however, and see that the master teaches and practices the same thing, it is possible to attain his qualities and become like him. It is all a question of how open we are. It is said that if we see the Buddha as an ordinary man, we will get the blessing of an ordinary man, while if we see an ordinary man as the Buddha, we will get the blessing of a Buddha. When experiencing things on the purest level, the mind will be open and its latent powers will develop, while in a skeptical mood, we can spend eons with Enlightened beings without noticing it. At the time of the Buddha, there was a monk who spent 40 years with him and learned nothing at all. He was convinced that the only difference between the Buddha and himself was the fact that the Buddha would shine at night.

The teacher is the one who opens the treasury of the Dharma to us. Though truth was never separate from the true essence of our mind, we need a teacher for this to become thoroughly clear in a lasting way. Like a mirror, he shows us our face, and from the ocean of teachings, he takes exactly that cupful which is most useful to us, here and now.

We move through three levels of devotion; initially confidence arises, then we strive, and, finally, there is no doubt. Here, devotion won't increase if the Lama sits on a high throne, and it won't decrease if he does something unpopular, such as shaking people out of their beloved mixed spirituality. One is certain that he knows what he is doing. Even in our lineage, some of the best people have had difficulties with this highest form of devotion, which requires giving up even one's precious "superior" knowledge. Milarepa, though he was able to stand his own purification so well, was totally depressed when Marpa asked him to make a hailstorm again. He picked up an armful of mice and birds that had been killed by the hail and took them to Marpa, saying, "Now you've brought me a lot of bad karma." Marpa answered, "Is that really so?" snapped his fingers and everything returned to life and scuttled away.

For a teacher to do unusual or seemingly harmful things, he must have the power to transform any damage and master all their effects. Thus, working outside ordinary morality necessitates certain powers. Without them, it's best to do what is generally useful and understandable, and to avoid scandal at all cost, especially today in the West where Buddhism is just becoming known.

As our confidence grows, the blessing of the Lama grows as well. Our inhibitions fall away and we can act meaningfully. Working hard, our "best attempts" become ever more guided; we are now inside the transmission and our lives have become more than just personal. If we keep

our bonds, say our KARMAPA CHENNOs, help the local
center and make sure that our motivation is right, we have
the security that the energy-field of the Karmapa will guide
us, even when we cannot see clearly ourselves.

"Non-distraction is taught to be the actual meditation
. . . grant your blessing that he may be free of 'something
to meditate on.'" Many of us, when first hearing about
meditation, get the idea that thoughts during practice are
something bad. This is a Hindu concept, not one of ours,
and thinking that way will only bring difficulties. At first,
we may be quite successful in sitting for a few minutes in a
thoughtless state, but then the first thought appears. If we
counter it by thinking: "I shouldn't think," there are already
two. Every attempt to force something will only make
things worse. It is therefore important to get the right
teaching on this point.

The state without thought is the space of the mind,
and thoughts are its clarity. Both are aspects of its unlimited
nature. A mind totally without thoughts is often dull or
sleepy, like a white wall, rather than radiant and diamond-
like. The Karmapas say very clearly that it's not a question
of thoughts or their absence but of staying naturally in what
is there. When we recognize the noises of the neighbor-
hood children for what they are, we can happily go on with
our work. In the same way, there's no need to be disturbed
when thoughts arise—we don't need to wish for good ones
to stay or bad ones to disappear, but instead, we just note
their playfulness, that their essence is ever fresh and new,
even when habitual or unpleasant thoughts come up again
and again.

We're not praying to be free of all thoughts, but rather

to not take them seriously or build up intellectual systems during meditation. The special thing about the Buddha's teaching, and what differentiates it from Christianity, Hinduism and non-Buddhist psychotherapy, is that we don't consider thoughts and conditioned feelings so important because they change all the time, anyway. Instead, we focus on the mind itself, which is timeless and absolute. Resting in this essence is what brings fearless-ness, joy and active compassion.

Whoever only "experiences," having no feeling for the experiencer, is at a disadvantage. This leads to pouring the free play of the mind into concrete molds and constantly evaluating thoughts as being good or bad instead of being bemused by their antics. What makes Buddhism ultimately liberating is its understanding that value systems are relative and that the only real thing is the mind itself. It recognizes the futility of trying to hold on to "good" states of mind or push "bad" ones away. It's much more useful to be aware that a certain problem wasn't there yesterday and will surely be gone tomorrow, and to put all power into what's necessary and natural, what's practical and in front of our nose. Then we aren't so dramatic about things, and in this way we can be effective even during the first years of our inner growth.

"The essence of thought is taught to be Dharmakaya . . . grant your blessing that he may realize the indivisibili-ty of Samsara and Nirvana." In the same way that the essence of waves is always the ocean, even though they manifest differently, the thoughts and the mind from which they arise cannot truly be separated. Everything, outer and inner, has the nature of "emptiness," is nothing in itself, but appears out of space, plays freely there, and then returns to space again. If we examine this body, our inner feelings and thoughts, the outer world and the situations there, we will find nothing which has any independent nature. Everything is interdependent, appearing from causes, changing, and dissolving again.

There are two ways to realize this emptiness or conditionality, but the experience is very different depending on whether it is understood intellectually or felt in our bones. In one Tibetan tradition, great debates are held about the emptiness of all things. People with an awakened emotional life, however, are initially left cold by this method. The result of intellectual analysis is that nothing *is*. Examining the conditioned world, we find that there is no "lasting" particle in the atom, nothing which really exists, that everything returns to space. Examining thoughts and feelings, we see exactly the same. They also dissolve again. Using only the intellectual level of the mind, a clear and logical view of the world appears which, unfortunately, brings little happiness to most people.

The meditation experience is different; it brings joy at once. Here, the whole mind is aware and we have both intuition and intellect. We experience space and clarity as inseparable. When every concept or object has disappeared, awareness still shines, fearless, joyful and compassionate. There is no "black hole" or nothingness; the seer doesn't disappear along with the thing seen. This is the joyful realization held forth by the yogis of the Karma Kagyu lineage. Our true essence is timeless and can never die; we are totally protected and secure, no matter what happens. Understanding this means really *living* the Refuge that we have.

Then we ask to understand that Samsara and Nirvana

are inseparable, that the basis of both is Mind. It's the way we see the world which makes things constricting or liberating.

The "Manam" prayer which now follows is well translated, but still I will add a few words. First one prays to the Lama in his essence as the Buddha and, after that, to his truth state, the Dharmakaya, which pervades all things; to his state of spontaneous joy, the Sambhogakaya; and to his active love, the Nirmanakaya. If we see Buddhahood as water, Dharmakaya would be the water vapor, Sambhogakaya, the clouds which condense out of that, and Nirmanakaya, the rain which makes all things come alive. All are aspects of a fully functioning mind and appear naturally on our way to enlightenment.

The statement that all beings have been our mothers is repeated to produce a strong feeling of gratitude. Sometime, somewhere, during our beginningless number of rebirths, all beings have done everything for us: nourished us, protected us and treated us as well as they could. Maybe, for Westerners used to abstract thinking, it would be more motivating to think that all beings share the same truth-nature and wish for happiness, but this is the traditional Tibetan way. More in books than in life, mothers, with their readiness to always give and be there for others, are considered very highly.

After the "Manam" prayers, which are repeated three times, come the Karmapa Chenno Mantras. There seems to be no fixed number to repeat, and so it's best to do what feels natural, maybe one Mala. During our daily lives, we should keep KARMAPA CHENNO in our mind whenever possible, but here, the function of the Mantra is to lead up to the next lines which we also repeat 111,111 times.

This is the last repetition in the Ngondro, and I advise paying close attention to the text's meaning and to really be aware of the fantastic things we will be repeating in Tibetan. We ourselves, as Dorje Phagmo, holding our Refuge, the golden Transmission Lineage, above our heads, and inspired through the former prayers, now open ourselves to Enlightenment.

We begin with "Lama Rinpoche la sol wa deb," which means "I pray to you, precious guru," and, after that, we wish: "Grant your blessing that my mind may let go of the belief in a self." This means that we will no longer see everything from the standpoint of a separated ego, that all disturbing feelings will become rootless, taking harmful actions, words and limiting habits along, and effectively stopping all suffering forever.

Next is: "Grant your blessing that desirelessness may be born in me." Instead of hoping for thousands of things, we wish to be satisfied with what comes naturally.

There was once a man who meditated in a cave with a great bush in front of the entrance. Whenever he walked in or out, he always got stuck on its thorns, and, each time, he would promise himself to borrow an ax somewhere to take it down. As soon as he was in the cave again, however, he would always think, "I really don't have the time; I can die any moment." And so he kept meditating. It is said that the bush is still there but the man got enlightened!

When we weigh the activities which "absolutely" have to be performed, we find that there is no end to them. More and more things appear for us to do, and we become richer, more famous and also older. Then one day we die and can bring none of it along. Therefore, being satisfied with little allows the free space for lasting, meaningful acts, such as meditation and working for the Dharma, to appear.

Then we wish: "Grant your blessing that non-Dharma thoughts may cease." This is what is called Namtok in Tibetan. It's the inner dialogue which is so difficult to stop, the steady flow of feelings and thoughts which have no meaning or power. It's all the whys and hows, the habits and doubts which make direct experience of things difficult. The traditional texts give several ways of getting rid of them which we can summarize as: avoiding, seeing as a dream, and just being aware. My "modern" advice is to keep them on an oily film of Mantras so that they float through the system and out the moment they appear. Another method is to catch them as one catches a thief and make them work, washing the car or tidying the garden; every time they appear, we use their energy for whatever needs doing, especially for the more tedious tasks. With the great blessing of the Lineage on the one side, activated through our prayer, and such skillful methods, there is no way that mental disturbance will not diminish.

"Grant your blessing that my mind may be realized as unborn." The first prayers were really for good behavior and taught us what is relative: that illusion brings suffering, while insight pays off; that non-Dharmic thoughts are harmful, and so on. Here, however, we come to the exciting wishes which take us beyond concepts and into the Mahamudra realm. We wish to realize that the clear light of the mind is its true nature, Perfection itself.

"Grant your blessing that delusion may subside of itself." The Mahamudra insight is expressed through its own power. This corresponds to the above mentioned level of "being aware" and means not to fight thoughts, not to use other thoughts as an antidote to those already present, but rather to let awareness liberate their inherent wisdom so that the mind's clarity can manifest through its concepts and fantasies.

"Grant your blessing that phenomenal appearances may be realized to be the Dharmakaya." This means seeing the conditioned world as truth. Nothing is separated from truth. On the absolute level, everything is true just by being there. Samsara and Nirvana are not different; the Pure Land is here right now. Repeating these wishes 111,111 times is such a massive influence that no matter how thick the ego is, something will get through and fixed concepts will be dissolved.

Finally, we invoke the Lama with devotion until we feel blessing. "Glorious perfect gurus, please grant me the four empowerments that bring spiritual maturity." What are the four initiations which help us to grow? First we have the Bumpeg-wang, or Vase initiation, the transmission which gives the power to experience our own body as that of a Buddha. During an initiation, this happens when we are touched on the top of our head with a small metal vase or are given something to drink from it. The vase contains the Buddha-aspects we're being initiated into and what we drink is their nectar or essence. This strongly purifies the energy of the body and makes it possible to be reborn as a Tulku. This level represents the Nirmanakaya.

The second empowerment is called the Sang-wang. It is the secret or speech initiation which happens when we repeat a mantra after the Lama or meditate that a chain of syllables streams out from him and dissolves into us. Here our inner energy channels are purified and the seed is planted for experiencing the state of joy to do the Six Yogas of Naropa. We call this state the Sambhogakaya.

The third transmission is called Sherab-Yeshe wang, and this wisdom-awareness initiation sows the seeds for sharing the mind of the Buddha aspect, the Dharmakaya, and for doing union-practice. It often happens through the attributes of the Enlightened form melting into us.

Finally, there is the fourth empowerment called the Tsig wang. Some translate it as the word initiation, others as the no-word. This gives us the seed of Mahamudra and may occur through the teacher simply resting for a moment, mixing his mind with ours, or through something he does or says which explodes every concept.

These are the four initiations, and with them we have now received the basis for seeing body, speech, and mind and the essence of all things as being pure. We have entered a Buddha-field and should now maintain this level of consciousness.

Our final prayer is for the power to express the four Buddha activities. In the same way that the sun doesn't want to shine, but does so because that is its nature, Enlightened activities spontaneously and effortlessly arise from radiant space, pacifying, maturing, magnetizing and powerfully protecting beings. To an active person, this last prayer may be the most inspiring of all, and we deeply wish to be able to do the work of the Buddhas in the world.

The Refuge now dissolves in light and melts into the Karmapa. And, as the essence of all Enlightenment, he either stays above us for more devotion or comes in front of us to give more clarity.

A shortened version of our Three Lights Karmapa meditation now fuses all this in the deepest levels of the mind. The white light to our forehead transfers the blessing of his body; the red light to the throat, the blessing of his speech; and the blue light to the center of our chest at heart-level, the blessing of his mind. All three together give his totality, the essential state of Mahamudra, Karmapa's timeless nature.

We may stay longer or shorter with the lights, after which the Karmapa melts together with us. Our body, speech and mind become inseparable from the Diamond body, speech, and mind of the Lama.

This can be done in different ways, but one that I find very useful sometimes is not letting the Karmapa dissolve, but rather, have his whole form come down over us and we directly become him. Instantaneously, we are then the Karmapa with all his abilities, surrounded by his Pure Land. Everything shines and sparkles; every atom vibrates with joy and is held together by love; everything has blessing, meaning, and essence. Seeing everything on the level of the Karmapa is the quickest way to spontaneous Enlightenment.

Finally, we share the merit. The word "Dharmata," used here, means "emptiness." The three diamonds—the indestructible essences of body, speech and mind—their realization is the whole reason for our way.

After Ngondro, I advise a year or more of meditating

on the Tun Shi Lami Naljor of the 8th Karmapa Mikyo Dorje; after that, both the ways of Naropa and Maitripa are open to you, leading to the great Mahamudra. Please learn from the great Teachers of the Karma Kagyu lineage and stay in contact with our centers. If there are none near you, we will gladly help you start one or support your individual work.

I wish you much sweat and joy.

A Partial List of Karma Kagyu Centers

UNITED STATES

Karma Triyana Dharma Chakra
352 Mead Mt. Rd.
Woodstock, NY 12498
(914) 679-2487
Seat in N. America of
H.H. Karmapa

Karma Dechen Oser Ling
P.O. Box 2426
San Anselmo, CA 94960
Laurel Bellon: (415) 653-9295
Asha Gilbert: (415) 826-9542
Ole Nydahl's main center in USA

Arizona

KTC c/o Erma Pound
6231 E. Exeter Blvd.
Scottsdale, AZ 85251
(602) 838-1066

California

Mt. Shasta KTC
c/o Maggi Starr
1431 Vista St.
Mt. Shasta, CA 96067
(916) 926-3955

Palo Alto KTC
P.O. Box 60793
Palo Alto, CA 94306
(415) 323-7944

Santa Barbara KTC
841 Mission Canyon Rd.
Santa Barbara, CA 93105
Janice Chase: (803) 682-4169

Kimberly Snow & Barry Spacks
1111 Bath St.
Santa Barbara, CA 93101
(805) 965-4944

Santa Cruz KTC
P.O. Box 8059
Santa Cruz, CA 95061
Lama Dudjom Dorje:
(408) 476-0651 / 462-3955

San Diego KTC
Carolyn & Van Hudson
13005 Caminito Mar Villa
Del Mar, CA 92014
(619) 755-3941

Colorado

Marianne Marstrand
P.O. Box 339
Crestone, CO 81131
(719) 256-4698 / 256-4694

Kentucky

Wayne & Jean Schmiedeknecht
676 Beth Lane
Lexington, KY 40503
(606) 223-4183

New Mexico

Bob & Melani Sachs
214 Girard Blvd. NE
Albuquerque, NM 87106
(505) 265-4826

KTC c/o Stan Witson
1030 Galisteo
Santa Fe, NM 87501

New York

Lisa Yannios
23-72 36th St.
Astoria, NY 11105
(718) 278-7452

Oregon

Marta Traister
7555 Rapp Lane
Talent, OR 97540
(Ashland area)

DENMARK

Karma Drub Djy Ling
Svanemollevej 56
2100 Copenhagen
01-292711

WEST GERMANY

Hamburg KCL
Harkortstieg 4
2000 Hamburg 50
W. Germany
040-389-5613

Schwarzenberg
c/o Kurt Nubling
Hinterschwarzenberg 8
D-8967 Oy-Mittelberg
W. Germany
49-8366-897